CULVER CITY

CHRONICLES

JULIE LUGO CERRA

Charleston London

THE
History
PRESS

Published by The History Press
Charleston, SC 29403
www.historypress.net

First published 2013

Manufactured in the United States

ISBN 978.1.60949.777.4

Library of Congress CIP data applied for.

CONTENTS

3. The Business of Building and Development

4. The Movie Studios

5. Education

6. Entertainment, Cultural Resources and More Lasting Memories

Contents

ACKNOWLEDGEMENTS

It all started with a favor in 1979, when my mother asked if I would take my dad to a Culver City Historical Society formation meeting. Daddy had flunked retirement three times, and he clearly needed more than golf. Mother declared, "He'll be a natural!" And she was right.

This presented an opportunity to enjoy time with my dad and learn more about the Lugo family heritage, which started in California in 1774. Born on the Lugo Ranch in 1908 in what would become Culver City, my father had a unique perspective and much to offer. Little did I know that we would become founding society members and take leadership roles with total family involvement.

Special thanks to Steve Hadland for the opportunity to write "Ask Julie" (which transitioned into "Looking Back") columns for the *Culver City News*. This anthology is culled from more than four hundred of those articles.

I am especially grateful for family support in this quest for knowledge of what my little brother Carlos calls the "olden days." We have learned firsthand from many early settlers and their descendants. My husband, Sam, used to proof work for me, but that task has fallen to my very literate and bright daughter Michele, who was our youngest tour guide. Michele, her husband, Kevin, and little Nicholas offer fabulous family support.

Thanks to Steve Rose and the Culver City Chamber of Commerce, which gave me the opportunity to write my first book; Darrell Fusaro for the opportunity to interview for *Local History, Legends and Lore*; the Culver City Historical Society for keeping me interested and making me stretch with Living History Programs; and the *Culver City News* for opportunities to broaden my horizons. And thanks to Aunt Jean Barker, Fred "Cuz" Machado, the Culver family—especially Robert Battle—and locals like June Caldwell, Martha Sigall, the Pittis, Ray Moselle, Stu Freeman and Marc Wanamaker, who have shared their stories and photos and answered many questions. A special thanks to the city for access to records.

INTRODUCTION

Culver City boasts a rich history, from the Native Americans and early settlers to visionary Harry H. Culver's dream for a balanced community through development and major redevelopment. Culver City continues to thrive as the "Heart of Screenland." Just walk around downtown Culver City at lunchtime and you'll see that studio IDs are a reminder of the presence of the entertainment industry and its broad base of support. Although many locals still miss the MGM sign, Sony Pictures Entertainment has been an extraordinary corporate citizen for more than twenty years.

The Gabrielinos used this land with respect, leaving fertile ground for the generations of early settler families like the Machados, Talamantes, Higueras, Ybarras, Saenz, Rochas, Lugos and others.

Statehood and other changes yielded new opportunities that city founder Harry Culver noted and used to develop the kind of community that brought families together in his "Home City." Culver's business acumen laid the foundation for an economic base that ensures a good, solid life with all the amenities.

Harry Culver's leadership brought people to a temperate place halfway between the growing pueblo of Los Angeles and Abbot Kinney's resort of Venice. He planned for success and the promise of a little community growing out toward the big city.

This is the story of the many people who shared the common goals that have yielded Culver City—an oasis within the urban metropolis and a city with a rich history.

CHAPTER 1

THE EARLY TIMES

OUR NATIVE AMERICANS

There was evidence of life in this area dating back to about 6000 BC. Some attribute the arrival of those early peoples to the land bridge that existed across the Bering Strait. However, there is little definitive evidence showing those ancients as the forebears of the Gabrielinos who inhabited this coastal area at the time of Spanish discovery and settlement.

The Native Americans we think of as local were called the Gabrielino Indians due to their proximity to the San Gabriel Mission, which was established in 1771. In all probability, their ancestors migrated from what became Oregon and Nevada through California deserts. They were Shoshonean (of Uto-Aztecan linguistic stock) and had impressive vocabularies, according to some. Because their history was passed down by word of mouth and since they lost their native languages in the colonization of California, our interest is often far greater than definitive information.

The Gabrielinos were social, peaceful people who lived in villages in Los Angeles (Yang-na) and Playa del Rey. They settled areas along water and lived in families (less organized than tribes) in huts called *jacals* or *wickiups*. These dome-shaped structures were quite large, framed in willows and thatched with tule grass, which was plentiful along Ballona Creek. A hole in the roof allowed smoke to escape, and hanging partitions offered privacy, as more than one family often lived together.

An artistic representation of the legend of Torovim, a Tongva chieftain who fled an enemy tribe by jumping from a cliff into the ocean and changing into a dolphin, or *torovim*, their brother in the ocean. This artwork was unveiled on April 28, 2000, on a cliff at Loyola Marymount University overlooking the ocean to commemorate that legend with the further explanation that the dolphin swims around the world as a protector and caretaker of the ocean.

La Ballona Valley offered water, safety and an abundance of food. The Gabrielinos constructed reed boats called *bolsas* or wooden plank canoes, both sealed with asphaltum from the location nearby known today as the La Brea Tar Pits or from deposits on the sandy beaches. They settled on high ground but moved through areas like ours to gather food. The Gabrielinos were also expert basketmakers. They constructed baskets for their everyday needs, including cooking acorns, which required the use of hot rocks in the water. They waterproofed their baskets with the same asphaltum used on the boats.

Acorns were considered the Gabrielinos' consistent food staple, but these Native Americans also hunted small animals, dug edible roots and picked berries. Acorns were gathered by the community at large and stored. After cracking and shelling them, the Gabrielinos made acorn mush by pounding them and then leaching the bitter acid from them in hot water. Beyond acorns, food gathering and preparation was mostly divided by gender. The elderly women and children generally gathered plant materials, seeds, beans and roots. Seeds were gathered using a beater that knocked them into flat baskets. They also ate pine nuts, walnuts and the fruits of cactus.

Hunters were usually male, except in the case of community rabbit hunts. These small animals were trapped into nets by large cooperative hunting parties. The Gabrielino men smoked out burrowing animals and then snared them or killed them with throwing sticks. Nets were also used to catch ducks and geese. The men also hunted coyotes, rodents, tortoises and lizards with slings, while hunting larger animals like deer, elk and mountain sheep required bows and arrows or spears. It appears that dogs were used to assist large hunting parties in this area, unlike in Mexico, where dogs were food.

Fish was a normal part of the Gabrielino diet. Small schools of fish were caught in nets. La Ballona Creek, lagoons (at Playa del Rey) and the swamps (*cienegas*) were ready sources of small fish. They also fished from the shore with line and abalone or bone hooks. Gabrielinos also used board boats and canoes that carried from three to thirty men. Although they hunted sea lions and seals (with spears and harpoons), whales were not generally hunted on the southern coast of California. However, stranded whales did occasionally provide meat and bone.

Most of the cooking occurred outdoors and was divided. Meats and fish were roasted in deep pits on hot coals, boiled or sun dried for future use. Shellfish were often steamed in pits layered with hot coals and seaweed and topped with sand. Soup was made from small animals that had been crushed. Tortillas were common, and grasshoppers were roasted on sticks in the same way that we toast marshmallows today.

The Gabrielino diet was partially dictated by availability and tradition. For example, bears, rattlesnakes and owls were often considered taboo. Other food restrictions were ceremonial. New mothers fasted and drank only warm water. New fathers also fasted and were not permitted to fish or hunt. Hunters fasted during the hunting party and were expected not to eat their own catch. There were special foods and drink prepared for initiation ceremonies for boys and girls at puberty.

Gabrielino rituals governed their daily lives. There were ceremonies for marriage, pregnancy, birth, puberty and death. Solstice was also a time of celebration. Cremation was common practice. Their chiefs, the primary leaders, acted as advisors and keepers of the sacred objects and calendar but received assistance from the heads of families and shamans, who were highly respected but often feared and enjoyed great political and religious power. There is evidence that women served in the capacity of shaman.

Families fell into classes, with the chief's family at the top of the hierarchy. Although they were monogamous, there was a process for divorce. Reasons included a barren or unfaithful wife. The husband of an unfaithful wife had the option to take the wife of her lover. Duties of the Gabrielinos were clearly defined, with cooking and housekeeping chores assigned to the women. Older women cared for the children, who learned their life duties early.

The Gabrielinos were short and stocky by today's standards. They had dark brown (not necessarily black hair), which was generally worn long and often pulled back in braids or ponytails. They wore scant clothing during the summer. To weather the winter cold, they wore skins and fabric. Tattoos were also common. Tradition called for girls' first tattoos between their eyebrows, progressing down their faces over the years.

Before the Spaniards arrived, Gabrielinos had their own system of money. When they were not hunting and preparing food, they spent time playing games, gambling and manufacturing goods like baskets (for which they were well known) and other objects like shell hooks and wooden and stone implements.

THE EARLY SETTLERS

The next settlers in this area came through Sinaloa, Mexico. José Manuel Machado married in Los Alamos and traveled to Alta California with his wife. Machado, a poor muleteer, enlisted as a *soldado de cuera*, or leather jacket soldier, dreaming of a better life. Muleteers had poor reputations, so Machado had to wait to marry María de la Luz Valenzuela Y Avilas until the church could determine that he had no other "intended." The Machados married in 1780 and traveled in Rivera's 1781 expedition to Alta California. José Manuel Machado retired in 1797 to the pueblo of Los Angeles, where his last child was born. After his death in 1810, two of his sons, José Agustín and José Ygnacio, tried unsuccessfully for some time to garner land near the pueblo.

In 1819, Agustín and Ygnacio Machado joined with Felipe Talamantes and his son Tomás to claim grazing rights to fourteen thousand acres of land. The family lore relates that Agustín, by virtue of his skill as a horseman, rode from dawn until dusk from the foot of the Playa del Rey hills to claim Rancho La Ballona, or *Paso de las Carretas*. The land stretched

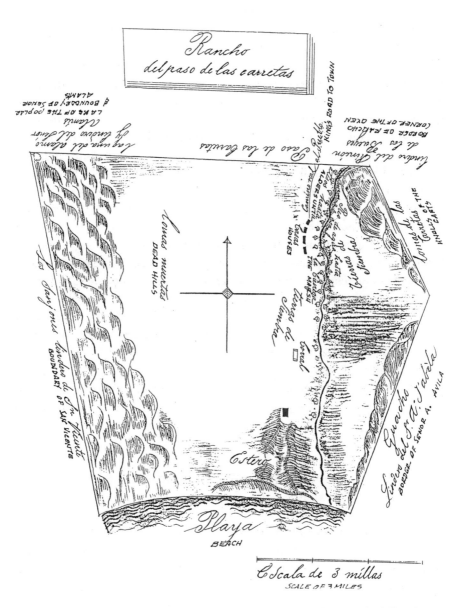

A *diseño* (map) of Rancho La Ballona. Note the north boundary of the rancho is Rancho San Vicente, Sepulveda property, while Avila land is south. The mapmakers were reliant on natural boundaries and markers.

from the ocean to what we now call Ince Boulevard, where Rancho Rincón de los Bueyes was destined to begin, up to Pico Boulevard and back to the ocean (abutting Rancho San Vicente y Santa Monica). The name Ballona remains a word in question. Some postulate that it may be a misspelling of *ballena*, meaning whale, or Bayona, España, a home of Talamantes's ancestors.

The Machados' first adobe home on Ballona washed away in flooding creek waters. Agustín Machado rebuilt nearby, probably on today's Overland Avenue at Sawtelle or Jefferson. Initially, Agustín traveled from the pueblo to tend his grapevines and herds of cattle and horses. By the late 1820s, Ygnacio Machado had planted corn and six thousand grapevines at nearby Centinela Springs. The Talamantes family lived to the east, on Policarpio Higuera's Rancho Rincón de los Bueyes.

Agustín Machado married in 1824, but his wife, María Petra Buelna, died while giving birth to their first child, Juan Bautista. In 1826, Ygnacio Machado married Estefana Palomares. The following year, Agustín Machado married Ramona Sepúlveda, who in turn gave him another fourteen children: María Josefa Delfina, Martina, Vicenta Ferrer (my great-grandmother), José Domingo, José Dolores, María Ascencion, Susana, José Franciso, Bernardino, Candelaria Onofre, José Ramón Tomás, José Juan Rafael, Andres Manuel and José de la Luz de los Reyes.

In 1834, Ygnacio Machado built the Centinela Adobe. Although Ygnacio received clear rights to Centinela in 1844, he traded the land to Bruno Avila for a house in the pueblo and two barrels of brandy in 1849. The adobe is preserved, and the Centinela Valley Historical Society is the caretaker.

Agustín Machado took charge of the undivided Rancho La Ballona for the partners. He was respected and well known both politically and for his white wine. He often traveled to San Pedro to trade for luxury items from overseas. The Machados held their rancho and other land through three governments: Spain, Mexico and the United States. In 1873, five years after Agustín Machado's death, Rancho La Ballona's title was finally clear. The James Machado family donated the last linen partition map to be displayed at Loyola Marymount University. Ygnacio died in 1878. He and Estefana had seven children: Luisa, Versabe, María, José, Andres, Francisco and Rafael. There are still many Machado descendants in the area, and they traditionally get together for a Machado family reunion every year in the fall.

RECOLLECTIONS FROM THE AUTHOR

Culver City's last ranch house was the Lugo Ranch at 11010 Jefferson Boulevard. The house faced Jefferson at Cota. This small eighteen-acre ranch was a wedding gift to my grandparents, Mercurial and Rita Reyes Lugo, from my great-grandparents, Francisco Lugo and Vicenta Machado de Lugo. Vicenta Machado was a daughter of La Ballona's founder, Agustín Machado. My grandfather, Mercurial Lugo, was a descendant of Francisco Salvador Lugo, who came to California in 1774 with a Rivera expedition. He was also one of the soldiers present at the founding of the pueblo of Los Angeles in 1781. Mercurial Lugo farmed the land and became the *zanjero* (*sanjero*), or water overseer, of the Ballona Water Company. In other words, he regulated the water to ensure that the irrigation needs were met for the local ranchers.

Since my grandparents died prior to my birth, my recollections are primarily those of visiting Auntie Vicenta and her brother Uncle Frank, who still lived on the ranch in the early 1950s when I would visit. As one approached the ranch, there was a circular dirt/gravel driveway with a full-grown weeping willow in the center. Auntie told me that my dad planted that tree as a child. My father, the youngest of the eight Lugo children, used to sell ranch-fresh produce from their corn stand.

To me, the ranch house was very dark, shaded by a huge palm tree in front. As a child, I was impressed by the stonework on the corner columns and below the porch. The house's façade was a dark painted wood, covered in some areas with vines—probably ivy. In the living room, I recall an upright piano, which remains in the family today, and at least two windows from which you could see the Studio Drive-In screen across the street. The living room opened up into a big dining room with a massive oak table, fitting for a family with eight children. Behind the dining room was a large kitchen, heavy with the aroma of Auntie's cooking, which often included albondigas soup, fresh tortillas or grape jelly. There was a door to the old-fashioned bathroom on the left, and at the back of the kitchen, the door opened out to the fenced yard, where Auntie kept her dog, Lobo. The few bedrooms were on the left side of the house, but I only recall Auntie's room, which was originally my grandparents'. A hand-carved oversized wooden rosary, which remains in the family today, hung over her bed.

Although it was no longer a working ranch when I visited, I remember helping my aunt with chores, like putting the hose down gopher holes in

Family members ran the Lugo Ranch Corn Stand where locals stopped to buy fresh produce. Pictured circa 1930 are siblings Charles Reyes Lugo and Vicenta Reyes Lugo with their nephew, George Reyes Lugo, behind. The ranch house can be seen in the distance.

the lawn! Auntie leased the south end of the property (at Sawtelle) to a Mr. Wilson, who operated a driving range and small golf course. On Tuesdays, I had to finish my homework so I could take golf lessons there. I regret not paying better attention!

There was another tiny residence at the ranch, near the barn, probably where the "boys" slept when they were older. Other random memories include standing on the Jefferson frontage waving to Dwight D. Eisenhower when he drove past in a motorcade. "Ike" had a presidential campaign office in the Culver Hotel at one time. Sorting through my recollections of the Lugo Ranch reminds me of the importance of family. My father took us to visit often. It seemed like Auntie was always wearing an apron and my very gentle Uncle Frank his heavy work clothes. His favorite song was "Cielito Lindo," and he taught us other verses of his childhood like "Pico de Gallo," remembered mostly by the pinching of little hands.

"Pico de Gallo"

Pico de gallo,
De gallo montero,
Paso un caballero
Veniendo puchero.
Le pedi un poquito,
Para mi burrito.
No me quiso dar,
Me dio una patada,
Que me hizo volar
Hasta las puertas de
San Miguel.

Translation:

The rooster
from the mountains
passed a gentleman
selling puchero [a soup with vegetables for babies].
I, the rooster, asked for a little bit for my little burro.
He, the gentleman, didn't want to give me any
He gave me a kick
It made me fly past the doors of San Miguel.

The following "nonsense rhyme" was one Uncle Frank used to teach to his nieces and nephews:

Luna, Luna
Comiendo tuna,
Tirando las cascaras
en la laguna.

Rough translation:

Moon, Moon,
Eating prickly pear,
Throwing the skins
in the lagoon.

(Provided and translated by cousin Doreen Lugo Job)

Auntie Vicenta sold the Lugo Ranch property in the mid-1950s. It was the last of the old ranches in the city. R.J. Blanco developed the Studio Village Shopping Center on the site along with other developments in the area of the lower crest and "Studio Village." In his later years, my dad often enjoyed coffee at the Roll n Rye because it was near the location of the old ranch house and he felt "at home." The Culver City Historical Society marked the ranch as Historic Site No. 8. The bronze marker was purchased with donations in honor of Charles Reyes Lugo after he died in 1987.

LIFE ON THE OLD RANCHOS

If we lived during the time of the early settlers, in the 1800s, we might have lived in an adobe house. To make the adobe bricks, the rancheros combined dirt and water to make mud and then added straw. To ensure a perfect consistency, especially in the case of the missions and presidios, the soil was often brought in. The adobe bricks were laid out to dry in the sun after they were formed. Homes were constructed of the adobe bricks and then plastered or "finished" with more adobe. After the adobe structure was dry, it required a whitewash made from crushed seashells. This provided a lime coating. The roof was often made of wood and fastened by handcrafted square nails. Several smaller adobes usually accompanied a bigger one, for the owner of a rancho. Many families lived on each rancho, including extended family and those of the workers, some of whom were Native Americans.

Families were close, so children knew well their aunts (*tías*) and uncles (*tíos*). Families traveled together on horseback and in horse-and-buggies with *carretas* (carts) to other ranchos for celebrations. Daily life was very predictable— early to bed and early to rise to get the work done. Preparation for special celebrations such as weddings and other family gatherings often took days.

The early settlers had many children, who were an active part of the workforce on the ranchos and were educated by tutors. The first elementary school was built in La Ballona Valley in 1865. At the time La Ballona School was established, school was in session only seven months of the year. This shortened schedule accommodated farming duties. Girls, even into the early 1900s, rarely had the option to attend secondary schools. They worked at home.

The days on a rancho started before dawn, with everyone dressed and assembled in the living room (*sala*) for prayers. According to an account

The Machado Adobe, where one of the founders of Rancho La Ballona, Agustín Machado, lived with his family. The first adobe perished in floodwaters. This home was built farther from the creek, which meandered in those early days. *Courtesy of Fred Machado.*

by Jose del Carmen Lugo written in 1878, breakfast (*desayuno*) was eaten while it was still dark, and it was determined, as were all meals, by the wealth of the family and their workday chores. Wealthier rancheros might begin the day with Spanish chocolate made with milk or water and corn or flour tortillas with butter. Poorer people often had milk with a cornmeal porridge (*atole*). Others would have only beans, while those who could eat just two meals a day often started with a solid meal of roast or stewed meat with chiles, onions, tomatoes and beans. In the very early times, the Spanish settlers brought their foods, which meshed with the ways of the Indians and yielded the Mexican flavors common in California. Plates and utensils were scarce in early times, so the settlers used tortillas to scoop their food or make burritos.

The men were often on horseback all day, except when they broke for meals and sleep. These men were the *vaqueros*, or cowboys. Boys assisted their fathers while the girls helped the women in the kitchen, cooking on wood-burning stoves. Their herb gardens near the house supplied the seasonings for cooking as well as medicinal purposes. Girls also learned to be proficient seamstresses.

The Culver City Chamber of Commerce, now more than ninety years old, was the first to recognize the early settler families, first as honored guests at the Fiesta La Ballona in 1951 and later in the placement of a plaque in Victory Park in 1963. *From left to right*: Mayor Dan Patacchia, Amada Szanthoffer, Vicenta Lugo, Senaida Lopez, Jerry Talamantes, Carlo Machado, Ella Cheuvront, Senaida Sullivan, Clarita Marquez Young, Charles Lugo, Caryll Wild and former chamber president John Boyd.

Ranchos typically had apricot and other fruit and nut trees. Other crops included barley, corn, wheat, beans and other vegetables. The Machados were also known for their vineyards and fine wines and the cattle they grazed on Rancho La Ballona. Boys assisted in the branding of the herds and, in the very early times, often slept outside after they were about six years old. The brands, which were registered with the state, showed ownership of the animals. Crop irrigation was regulated by the *zanjero*. The Higueras also grazed sheep, which were sheared to make clothes. The early settlers traded their goods and services for others. They also took their goods to San Pedro to trade for luxury items.

In the 1800s, most men (except for soldiers) were clean-shaven and wore their hair long. Their hair was pulled back behind their ears and kept neat with a scarf or bandana and covered with a hat. Some tied their hair in a queue. They wore cotton shirts under their jackets, and their pants (*pantalones*) were cut just below the knees. Women wore skirts and blouses or dresses; shawls; and stockings. Their long hair was generally parted in the center, drawn back and often braided and pinned up. Wealthy landowners rode their horses in fancy outfits trimmed in silver on Sundays and special occasions. Marriage was arranged by parents, or at the very least, a man asked the father of his intended for her hand. This practice was still commonplace in the late 1800s.

Even after 1900, life was simple, with few luxuries. Clothing was more relaxed, and children attended school more, especially the boys. The boys and men worked the ranch and sold vegetables at their corn stand on Jefferson. My Auntie Vicenta washed and ironed for the family, which included a little sister and six brothers. At that time, there was still a clear division of labor in the household chores. She used her mother's recipe to make flour tortillas on the Lugo Ranch in Culver City. Although she cooked them over a wood-burning stove, the following recipe, which uses a cast-iron griddle, is still in family use today:

AUNTIE VICENTA'S FLOUR TORTILLAS

In a bowl, cut in shortening with a fork:
2 cups flour
pinch of salt
wwwwcup solid vegetable shortening (originally lard)

Add the following warm-water mixture a little at a time until dough is pliable.
Depending on the humidity and flour, you may only use ¾ cup total:
⅞ cup warm water
⅛ cup milk

Knead until elastic and then roll pieces into rounds the size of golf balls and place on a towel.
Cover with another towel.
Let set for at least 30 minutes.
Heat griddle.
Roll into nice, thin rounds using a floured board. Place on hot griddle until bubbles form, then flip the tortilla and cook on the other side.
Stack tortillas on a towel.
Makes 15–20.
Serve warm with butter or use for burritos or soft tacos!

BALLONA CREEK

Ballona Creek began as a picturesque natural waterway fed by runoff. The creek collected the water from *cienegas* and the rains. In early times, the banks were lined with trees such as sycamores, willows and tules, and even in the 1900s, locals collected watercress growing at the creek's edge for their families' salads. A natural resource for the indigenous people, the creek also became important to the early settlers, who used it as a source of irrigation water. City engineering employees like Sam Cerra verified stories of residents on Cota Street, near the creek, unearthing old pipes from those times.

The waterway continued as an important component of city history when Harry Culver noticed filmmaker Thomas Ince shooting one of his famous western movies on location at Ballona Creek. Culver subsequently made a deal to sell the land to Ince for a movie studio. Legend has it that Ince normally used the Los Angeles River, but this film required a smaller waterway for his painted Indians in a canoe.

The creek often became a source of frustration for the early Culver City trustees. On October 2, 1922, by Resolution No. 250, the governing body directed the city attorney to "take immediate legal steps to secure relief from the nuisance from the intolerable condition caused by failure of the City of Los Angeles to abate the nuisance in Ballona Creek." José de la Luz Machado (Agustín Machado's youngest son) lived on Overland Avenue between Jefferson and Farragut. His wife found it necessary to attend what we now call council meetings to complain, rather pointedly, of the same raw sewage. There were also the issues of the ranch boundary being moved by the creek and, in later days, chemicals.

La Ballona Creek's meandering ways eventually required the help of the U.S. Army Corps of Engineers. The corps came in, straightened it and made its course permanent by paving the sides of Ballona Creek in 1935. No more homes were lost.

As a child, Fred Machado swam in what he remembers as the clear waters of Ballona Creek. He can still picture the sides of it, lined with trees and tules and home to ducks and small fish. Fred still talks about their ranch house near Centinela and Jefferson, imparting that it was "built so high you could walk under it." This ranch was located on a Machado portion of Rancho La Ballona, just outside Culver City. Fred Machado is a direct descendant of Ballona founder Agustín Machado through the eldest son, Juan Bautista. Fred likened this accommodation for flooding and subsequent use of the rich silt deposits for farming to the rich soil provided along the banks of the famed Nile River. He recalled the flood on New Year's Day 1934, which exceeded helpful silt deposits and kept the family from tilling some of their ranch land ever again. From then on, it was impossible to grow castor beans, and according to Fred, the wild doves and rabbits also never returned. Fred's father worked as a mechanic on the dragline equipment that dug out the soil to straighten the creek. He was impressed by the crane, which had a sixteen-cubic-yard bucket on a dragline that moved on pontoons at one and a half to two miles per hour. He liked to go to work with his father at night and watch the operation.

Sometime after the creek was stabilized, it was lined with large rocks. The rocks were quarried on Catalina Island and brought by barge to the creek. The concrete was applied after the rocks were in place. Today, the creek falls under the jurisdiction of the U.S. Army Corps of Engineers, Los Angeles Flood Control and Los Angeles County Public Works, among other jurisdictions.

Locally, there are bridges over the creek at Washington Boulevard, Higuera, National, Duquesne, Sepulveda and Sawtelle. An assessment district paid for the first pedestrian bridge at Ocean Drive to transport students safely to schools, which was later replaced in a joint effort by the city and county. The creek has become the largest storm drain in the Santa Monica watershed. Today, it begins as a creek at Cochran, south of Venice Boulevard, and ends at the Pacific Ocean.

The Ballona Creek Renaissance Program works diligently to return the creek to a more aesthetically pleasing and functional waterway. In the meantime, Culver City participates in creek cleanups and enjoys the use of the bike path, which leads to the ocean. Artwork can be enjoyed near the entrances to the bike path near the Culver City Julian Dixon Library and Syd Kronenthal Park. The transportation facility at Duquesne has opened its front door to view the waterway.

SAENZ STORE

The first post office to serve Rancho La Ballona and Rancho Rincón de los Bueyes was situated on La Ballona in the Saenz family's dry goods store, and a Saenz family member served as the first postmaster. The location was basically today's intersection of Overland Avenue and Washington Boulevard. In early times, Overland was called the Road to San Pedro, and

The first post office in the area was the Machado Post Office, which was located within the Saenz family's dry goods store at the edge of what became Culver Center. This shows a partnership between the Saenz and Higuera families. *Courtesy of Michael Hennarty.*

Washington can be identified on old maps as El Camino del Paso de las Carretas. There is also documentation that indicates that Sy Saenz's boxing arena was located just west of the dry goods store on the property now known as the Culver Center. The Saenz family is among the early settlers recognized on a plaque in Culver City's first park, now known as Dr. Paul Carlson Park. The Culver City Garage, owned by Saenz, was located a short distance farther east on today's Ince and Washington Boulevards.

STATEHOOD AND CAMP LATHAM

Things changed when California was admitted to the Union in 1850. The early settlers did not understand interest rates, and many struggled to keep their land. Meanwhile, the Civil War yielded more than one camp in this area. Camp Latham, which existed from 1861 to 1862, was established by the First California Infantry, under Colonel James H. Carleton, and the First California Cavalry, under Lieutenant Colonel Benjamin F. Davis. Named for U.S. senator Milton S. Latham, who also served as California's sixth governor, this Union tent encampment was Southern California's initial staging area for the Civil War.

In early 1861, there was rising concern that California, which had just recently become a state, might fall to "Southern sentiment." It was to curb this spirit that a Union camp was established in Southern California. The soldiers—all volunteers—came primarily from middle or northern California. Sent by ship, they disembarked at San Pedro and walked a full day (eighteen miles) to establish a tent camp. Camp Latham was located on the south side of Ballona Creek on land that had been claimed by the Machado and Talamantes families in 1819 as their Rancho La Ballona.

Although references existed in some material, such as the Title Insurance's 1939 publication "Culver City: A Calendar of Events," the exact location of this camp has been difficult to define. In 1982, the Culver City Historical Society renewed the public's interest in the town's history by hosting a reenactment program featuring a Civil War Association unit from Fort Tejon. The only problem was finding the exact location, which was complicated by the meandering of La Ballona Creek before it was straightened and reinforced in 1935. In 2000, access to added materials reinforced Culver City's historic site chairman Sam Cerra's research on the location of Camp Latham. A bronze marker is now located at Rotary Plaza at Virginia and Overland Avenues. It appears that more than 1,500 volunteers were stationed at Latham during its short existence. There were also brick ovens for a bakery and a smaller camp, Camp Kellogg, located across the creek to the north.

Many ask, "Who was Camp Latham named for?" Milton Slocum Latham was born in Ohio in 1827 and educated in Pennsylvania. He later served as a schoolteacher, court clerk and lawyer. Arriving in California in 1850 (California's admission year), he served as a district attorney, U.S. representative and collector for the Port of San Francisco. Interestingly, Latham was a "Lecompton Democrat," a party known for its pro-South stance. His election to the governor's seat was opposed by many who feared he would turn California into a pro-slavery state. In most material, references are more common to Senator Latham—not governor. It appears that at that time, senators ranked higher in status than governors. Latham supposedly ran for governor because he wanted the seat of Senator Broderick, who had been killed in a duel. Governor Milton Latham was the only governor known to keep a daily diary of his time as governor—but that was easier than most since he held that office for only five days!

Camp Latham preceded Camp Drum in San Pedro, which was later known as Drum Barracks and generally considered California's main tie to the Civil War. Camp Drum has the distinction of being the location of the "Camel Experiment"—an unsuccessful dromedary courier experiment to the Mojave Desert that lasted two years.

FIRST SCHOOL AND CHURCH

La Ballona School, originally a wood-frame structure, held its first classes as a part of the Ballona School District in 1865–66. In the school's first year, there were seventeen boys and eleven girls. The teacher, Miss Craft from Boston, received fifty dollars a month, including board. The school year lasted just seven months so that children could also work on the ranchos. Established on a portion of Rancho La Ballona, this is the oldest school in what became Culver City. It eventually became a part of the Culver City Unified School District (CCUSD).

The early Spanish settlers attended Mass either at the Old Soldiers' Home at Sawtelle or else rode to St. Monica's in Santa Monica. Both were considerable trips by horse-and-buggy. La Ballona Valley residents grew in number, and in 1883, a prominent landowner, J. Francisco Figueroa, donated acreage to the diocese of Los Angeles for the construction of a new mission church. The little white wood-frame church faced Washington Boulevard, then a dirt road. The new church, served by priests from St. Monica's, was named St. Augustine's, for the son of St. Monica. Father Patrick Hawe, the pastor of St. Monica's, built the mission church and came to hold Mass there. Participants grew in number, and Father Hawe began to share duties with priests from St. James in Redondo Beach and St. Clement in Ocean Park. The mission church seated about two hundred.

In 1919, two years after Culver City was incorporated, it was necessary to appoint a permanent pastor for St. Augustine's, which would become a parish of the Monterey–Los Angeles Diocese. The first resident pastor, Father Thomas O'Toole, was appointed on November 30, 1919. During Father O'Toole's two-year tenure as pastor, he built the first rectory (priest's house), which was moved to Jean Place in 1926 for a convent. Each

La Ballona School was the first school built in what became Culver City. This initial wooden structure was followed by one of concrete and then brick, respectively. The site was marked by the Culver City Historical Society.

The first St. Augustine's Church was built in the 1880s on property donated by the Figueroa family. Though the church is now in its third structure, it has always faced the studios across the street on Washington Boulevard. *Courtesy of Christina Machado Essex.*

subsequent pastor added something for which he was remembered. In 1922, the new pastor enlarged the church to seat 500. In 1926, the little parish hall was converted into a four-room schoolhouse, and a new stucco rectory was built. The Daughters of Mary and Joseph were invited that year to staff the school. They arrived on the Feast of St. Augustine, August 28. The staff of 6 sisters opened St. Augustine's School within two weeks with an initial enrollment of 123.

In 1936, a new St. Augustine's Church was constructed with a seating capacity of seven hundred. Erected by noted church builder Don Ely, the bird-cage-like steel-frame structure caused a stir as it was woven into a single unit. Ely also built the American Legion Building, now Brotman Medical Center's Glantz Auditorium, on Hughes Avenue. The new church was dedicated in April 1937 by Archbishop John J. Cantwell of Los Angeles. The pastor, Father O'Donnell, often acted as a technical advisor to MGM Studios across the street. The studio often helped the church raise funds by putting up tents for the annual barbecue, for which the Machado family cooked the beef.

In 1947, a new school was completed, replacing the old bungalows with reinforced concrete, and the year after, a new convent was constructed. Father (later Monsignor) James McLaughlin became the pastor in 1949, and he not only added to the school but also supervised the building of the church in use today. Constructed by Pasadena's Theisen & Co., the fourteen-thousand-square-foot American Gothic structure was built to accommodate 1,070 parishioners. McLaughlin opened the doors as a surprise on Christmas Day 1957.

The present church was officially dedicated six months later by James Francis Cardinal McIntyre, archbishop of Los Angeles, on June 22, 1958, with standing room only. Throngs of dignitaries and locals attended the ceremony after hearing that a famous radio and television personality, Bishop Fulton J. Sheen, was coming from the East to preach. Bishop Sheen and Monsignor McLaughlin attended the seminary together.

The little mission chapel in La Ballona Valley is no longer there, but the second church is used as a parish hall alongside the new church. In addition to regular church work, the parish sponsors St. Augustine's Volunteers for Emergency Services (SAVES), a non-denominational entity that helps those in need. The city's irregular boundaries put St. Augustine's Church in Culver City, while the school sits in a portion of Los Angeles.

BALDWIN HILLS

The Baldwin Hills rose above Ballona Valley as a part of three ranchos: La Ballona, Rincòn de los Bueyes and La Cienega O Paso de la Tijera. The hills carry the name of a nineteenth-century buyer, Elias Jackson Baldwin, who purchased the third rancho and named it to reflect the natural pass, which resembled scissors (*tijera*). Baldwin, who was born in Ohio in 1828, came to California in 1853. A colorful character with money on his mind, Baldwin's life in California could be told "from poker, horse racing, mining shares, real estate and other less legitimate enterprises," according to Pryor's *Little Known Tales in California History*.

History is told in stories that resemble colorful overlapping transparencies. When E.J. "Lucky" Baldwin landed in San Francisco, his first few days were spent at the Pacific Temperance Hotel. As the story goes, Baldwin was sure he could do a better job of running the establishment. The proprietor told Baldwin he would sell the hotel for $6,000, to which the visitor countered with a $5,000 offer. After three days of negotiating, the two men came to an agreement for $5,000, with the stipulation that Baldwin could backdate the check three days to impress the folks back home. After signing the papers, the new owner mentioned the pending matter of Baldwin's three days' boarding. The former owner was delighted, thinking that he would be collecting three days' fare, but Baldwin reminded him that technically he had owned the hotel for three days, so it was Baldwin who would be collecting for the three days! Within a month, Baldwin had sold the hotel for twice what he had paid, and so began the story of E.J. "Lucky" Baldwin in California.

When Baldwin came to Southern California, he was enamored with Rancho Santa Anita, and he began to negotiate the sale of the oak-studded ranch once owned by the legendary Hugo Reid. Santa Anita, just east of today's Pasadena, was about twelve square miles with an ocean view. Baldwin purchased the rancho in 1875 from Los Angeles businessman H.L. Newmark in another well-known transaction story. In the end, it cost him $175,000 ($90,000 more than Newmark had paid), and the initial $12,500 payment came out of a tin box under Baldwin's arm, which reportedly held millions of dollars. Legend has it that Baldwin's interests (other than money) included women and horses, and I think there was something about "fast" in there too. Baldwin lived and bred champion racehorses on Santa Anita, developed Arcadia and established his dream racetrack on the property in 1907. Although this first racetrack was short-lived, Culver City's studio head, Hal Roach, was instrumental in founding the current Santa Anita Race Track that opened on Christmas Day 1934.

When Lucky Baldwin died in 1909, his estimated income had reached $200,000 a month. He was worth $200 million, but during his adventurous career, he rarely paid a debt without being nudged by a court judgment. Oil was not found in the Baldwin Hills until the mid-1920s, at which point the land was part of the estate of Baldwin's daughter, Clara Baldwin Stocker. That explains the naming of Stocker Street, too.

An often-asked question involves a legend that the two-story house at the top of the Baldwin Hills across from Kenneth Hahn Park (west of La Cienega) was built by *Los Angeles Times* publisher Harry Chandler for his mistress. Ray, the home's longtime caretaker and one of the few people with memories of the inside of the house, has since passed away. But we do have a firsthand account from Fred Machado, who saw the house a few times with a retired Culver City fireman. Machado described Ray, who had been there about twenty or thirty years, as a colorful "cowboy-type character." He thought the house had been built about 1900 and noted that it was a two-story wooden house, almost Craftsman-like on the outside and Victorian on the inside. He was struck by the original fixtures, which had been converted to gas, and a claw-foot bathtub. Fred recalled that it had a basement and that the first floor was "good-sized," about two thousand square feet. There were oil wells in the front yard of the house—one of the six Machado leases, in fact.

Well-known developer Fritz Burns and his partner, Fred Marlow, purchased some of the swampland known as Rancho La Cienega from Clara Baldwin Stocker to develop Windsor Hills. Inglewood Field was the Baldwin land set aside for oil drilling by Standard Oil (Chevron), Getty Texaco and Shell. Fritz Burns called this land the "luckiest investment Lucky Baldwin ever made."

One of many quotes about Southern California attributed to Lucky Baldwin related to real estate: "Hell, we're giving away the land. We're selling the climate." Today, this historic land hosts some wonderful park space.

IVY SUBSTATION

The Ivy Substation was constructed in 1907 by the Los Angeles Pacific Railway, which later became part of the Los Angeles Pacific Railway Electric Company. One of the railway's largest electric substations, it

The Ivy Substation is a local landmark in Los Angeles at the edge of Culver City. The substation was placed on the National Register of Historic Places by noted railroad historian David Cameron, who was also a member of the Culver City Historical Society.

served as a branch for the electrical generation and distribution system. Electricity was transformed and distributed to create the power for the electric railway system. The substation received alternating current (AC) and transformed it into direct current (DC) for use by the electric trains. It was located along the "Balloon Route" rail line from downtown Los Angeles to the Pacific Ocean.

When real estate developer Harry Culver searched the area to establish a city, an important factor was transportation. By the time Culver City began to materialize in 1913, one could catch a "Red Car" downtown to Los Angeles or to Abbot Kinney's resort of Venice. In fact, it was near the Ivy Substation that Harry Culver noticed his future wife, who was waiting to ride the Red Car downtown for a shopping trip. By 1954, the historic Mission Revival–style building stood empty, and eventually the weathered structure became a haven for transients. In the mid-1970s, David Cameron, a noted railroad historian, realized that the building must be protected or face demolition. Cameron, a member of the Culver City Historical Society, completed the application to place the Ivy Substation on the National Register of Historic Places. His successful campaign saved the structure from demolition during the Caltrans Venice Boulevard Improvement Project in 1981. The substation is also designated as Los Angeles Historic-Cultural Monument #182.

Although the structure actually lies in Los Angeles, Ivy Substation appears as a gateway to Culver City. Recognizing this, the Culver City Redevelopment Agency (CCRA) entered into a long-term lease with the City of Los Angeles in 1987 that included the adjacent Media Park. The renovation of the building and park was funded by the CCRA. Los Angeles retained jurisdiction over the properties with review by the Los Angeles Cultural Affairs Department and the Cultural Heritage and Cultural Affairs Commission. This also ensured that the renovation would comply with the standards established by the U.S. secretary of the interior.

Design and construction plans were prepared by architect Milford Wayne Donaldson, FAIA, who later served as a state historic preservation officer. The renovation, performed by Driver Eddy Construction Co., included asbestos abatement, lead-based paint removal, seismic strengthening of the original brick building, installation of replicated historic power poles and wires and the artistic cooling fountain, provision of utility services and ancillary facilities, non-intrusive disabled access modifications and landscaping improvements to the adjacent park grounds.

The Ivy Substation reopened during a week of community celebration in April 1993. Since that time, it has been used as a venue for a variety of entertainment events, meetings and parties. The Center Theatre Group transformed it into a performing arts facility while it was renovating the nearby landmark Culver Theatre, now Kirk Douglas Theatre. Since 2005, the Actors' Gang has been the resident theater company at the one-hundred-year-old historic Ivy Substation.

CHAPTER 2

CULVER CITY TAKES SHAPE

ENTER HARRY CULVER

Harry H. Culver was born in Milford, Nebraska, on January 22, 1880. He was the middle child of five, raised with three brothers and a sister on the family farm. Their father, Jacob Hazel Culver, was a National Guard brigadier general and strict disciplinarian descended from Englishman Edward Colver, who arrived in Massachusetts in 1635. Taking the lead from his father, Culver enlisted in the Spanish-American War. Although underage, he worked his way from trumpeter to sergeant. After a year at Doane College, he spent three years at the University of Nebraska. He financed his education through assorted jobs, including taking in laundry and going into the bottled water business with his father.

Culver traveled to the Philippines in 1901 and went into the mercantile business. He also worked as a reporter for the *Manila Times*. After a three-and-a-half-year stint as a special agent in the customs department, Culver returned stateside to customs special duty in St. Louis and Detroit. He resigned in 1910 to move to California. In Southern California, Culver took a job with I.N. Van Nuys in real estate. As the story goes, after Van Nuys offered to make him a manager because of his exemplary work, Culver decided to venture out on his own. After intense study, Harry Culver pinpointed the area between Los Angeles and Abbot Kinney's resort of Venice for his city. He announced his plans at the California Club in Los Angeles in 1913. He

City founder Harry Hazel Culver was born on January 22, 1880, in Milford, Nebraska. Although he was heralded as a visionary, his daughter felt "he simply knew what people wanted." *Courtesy of the Culver family.*

formed the Culver Investment Company and relocated his office from the Story Building in Los Angeles to Main Street, Culver City. Unlike in Palms, the locals rejected annexation to Los Angeles in 1914. Culver worked toward his goal of a balanced community.

After he watched Thomas Ince film a western on Ballona Creek, Harry Culver convinced Ince to move his studios from the beach (Inceville) to Washington Boulevard. The landmark colonnade was built in 1915, and Culver City, incorporated in 1917, was on the road to becoming the "Heart of Screenland."

During this exciting time, Culver was traveling around Media Park in his Pierce-Arrow. It was then that he first caught a glimpse of a striking young woman in a yellow suit and straw hat waiting for the Venice Short Line.

Lillian Roberts Culver holding Patricia, who was born on August 11, 1917. The statuesque Mrs. Culver took a hiatus from movies but acted in the theater and hosted a radio show before returning to work in the studios. *Courtesy of the Culver family.*

After inquiring who she was, Culver's chauffeur thoughtfully suggested, "She may be one of the new people." Culver's daughter Pat always enjoyed sharing the story of her parents' first meeting. Knowing their difference in age might be cause for concern, Culver spoke to the wife of a prominent doctor, who agreed to give a party for the "newcomers" in town. With the knowledge that the young woman was Lillian Roberts and was "well brought-up," Culver's friend Mrs. Jones asked Lillian's mother if she and Dr. Jones could take Lillian to a party. Harry Culver drove to the party at the shore with Dr. and Mrs. Jones in the back seat. Miss Roberts rode in the front seat with her admirer, and as Pat loved to say, "The die was cast." Harry Culver married the young actress Lillian Roberts in June 1916, and on August 11, 1917, Dr. Jones delivered their only child, Patricia.

Harry Culver's Dream: The 1913 Speech

Many have asked why Harry Culver chose this location. The answer lies in the speech he gave at the California Club on July 22, 1913. A reprint of Harry Culver's words to that gentlemen's club in downtown Los Angeles appeared in the October 31, 1914 issue of the *Culver City Call* with this comment:

Following is the text of the speech made about a year ago at a dinner at the California Club by Harry H. Culver announcing the birth of Culver City. The speech is worthy of reading again at this time in view of the wonderful success of Culver City in its past year.

Prophecy Fulfilled

"I Love You, California" has been re-echoed around the world, both in song and story. But no one can fully appreciate its meaning as much as the person who is fortunate enough to call California home. And to all true Californians, those magic words send a thrill similar to that which is experienced by all true Americans at the mention of the "Star-Spangled Banner."

California, besides its thousands of fertile acres that in the different sections will grow to perfection anything in plant life that can be raised anywhere on earth, its countless oil wells and mines of gold, silver and other metals, has within its confines more natural scenic attractions than any other equal area on the face of the globe.

It's a well-organized modern city with a population of 75,000, with banks and factories and stores great and small and millions of money with railroads and street railways, with sixty miles of solid, substantial, beautiful homes, with schools and churches, were to be picked up one fine day and moved intact and complete, people and all, onto vacant territory adjoining the city of Los Angeles, the whole world and particularly we of this city would be overwhelmed with wonder and amazement.

The event would become one of the marvels of the world. It would be discussed in all the languages. And it would go down in history as the most extraordinary event human mind ever struggled to grasp.

That very thing was done in the year which closed June 30. Of course, the people came in groups and carloads, and were assimilated gradually. The buildings came by train and ship, in the form of materials. The money came in from all over the world—$250,000 a day. The railways and railroads came with extensions of a few miles each month.

Very few realized what was being achieved in this city. All watched the growth with interest, but the recurrence of the story month after month dulled interest. This same growth goes on constantly. The sound of the hammer and the saw, the groan of derricks, the clatter of the riveter, the fall of the pile-driver, the whistle of engines, the gong of cars, saturate us benumb our minds. When the whole column of figures showing progress is totaled, we rub our eyes.

But do we grasp its significance? Does the world know what we are doing? Think, if you can, without confusion, of sixty-three solid miles of new residences in twelve months! Think of $33,000,000 expended in one year for buildings. Think of the post office receipts gaining $200,000 in one year. Think of a 20 per cent increase in all business in 365 days. Think of bank clearings of more than one billion dollars. Think of bank clearings of more than one billion dollars. Think of a manufacturing business of $100,000,000—and Los Angeles only just making the first feeble beginning as an industrial center! So the great prosperity of the last twelve months is a lesson as well as a source of pride and gratification. It has been wonderful, and the world is beginning to realize it.

What is the attraction, gentlemen? Climate. What makes possible the climate? That wonderful ocean. On a clear day, step out to the last home on Washington Street and gaze towards the ocean—and what do you see? Venice of America! A city built on the sands but as enduring as the hills because the very reason of its being is based on that play-spirit of the people.

To the casual observer, Venice is merely a gigantic amusement place, whose purpose is solely to draw the nickels and dimes of the people. This was probably the only outward reason for its creation, but unconsciously there must have been a realization of the city's great need.

Thousands and thousands of city dwellers, tired of apartments that you can fold up and tuck in your vest pocket; tired of great buildings that reach up to heaven but never get there; tired of the feverish madness of the marathon of gold; these thousands must play.

Therefore, Venice is the big playground. The cool ocean breezes blow away all mental dustiness as the big cars of the Pacific Electric flash through the twenty-three subdivisions that intervene between Los Angeles and Venice.

Venice may have been an inspiration, but the inspiration was handled by a mastermind. It is the nearest beach to the city of Los Angeles. That in itself is a big item, for minutes and seconds rise far above par when dealing with thousands and thousands of passengers.

There are already seven railroads, electric and steam, entering Venice and connecting it with Los Angeles and neighboring places. The question of a *subway must be taken up soon. This will mean shortening the time from Los Angeles to Venice by several minutes, and will enable the railroads to handle the crowds to much better advantage.*

When Venice was conceived there was nothing for the imagination to work upon but a stretch of sand and low, dark marshes. The same sand which sold for ten cents per load then is now valued at $1,500 per foot front. This has all been accomplished in eight years.

Gentlemen, for two years I have carefully watched a courtship maturing between these two cities—in fact, the "stork" has been busy, and at this time, I can't tell whether it's a boy or a girl, but I can certainly hope "it's a bear." If you draw a straight line from the Story building to the Ocean Front at Venice, at the halfway mark you will find three intersection electric lines—the logical center for what we propose to develop a townsite. We believe this is the time, place and the girl; and so the deal is going over. After the town has been christened, we propose to wage a selling campaign second to none in California for rapidity of sales. I believe I can count on every man present here this evening to boost the proposition, and as a result the new-born town will have a successful career, and be a credit to the community as well as to the men associated with me in its development.

A Fork in the Road: Palms and Culver City

Just as "no man is an island," one could extrapolate that to our communities. Palms was an early designation and, at one time, even included some of the land that became Culver City. For example, Charles Lugo's 1908 birth certificate read, "Baby Lugo, Palms." He was actually born in the Lugo Ranch house (Cota and Jefferson), the last of eight children and the only one to be shown into this world by a doctor.

According to W.W. Robinson's 1939 publication for Title Insurance and Trust, Palms was subdivided in 1886 by Joseph Curtis, E.H. Sweetser and C.J. Harrison. The palm trees came later, by all accounts. In 1914, the people in this area, originally a part of Rancho La Ballona, were offered an opportunity to become part of the pueblo of Los Angeles. The electorate in

A 1920s view of Palms from the perspective of real estate professionals at Schilling Anderson Real Estate, which was located on the northeast corner of Motor and Venice Boulevards. *Courtesy of June Anderson Caldwell.*

Palms voted to do just that. But Culver City residents already had a strong identity, and they decided to become a city on their own. Voters had multiple decisions to make in 1917—if Culver City was to become an incorporated city, trustees, a clerk and a treasurer must be elected. These choices appeared on the same ballot.

After Harry H. Culver's 1913 announcement, people began to learn of his innovative sales techniques. He was considered a marketing genius in real estate, and he used promotions to give the new city maximum exposure. His well-known events included bus rides, free picnic lunches, "prettiest baby contests" (with a prize of a Culver City lot), klieg lights and a marathon race. He also put ads in the local papers that read, "All Roads Lead to Culver City."

Harry Culver's marathon was a 1913 dream that would be realized a year later. His motivation was publicity, and it was well executed. Early records show that a cavalcade of cars followed the runners, who numbered sixty in the first year. Pathè News covered the event to broadcast nationwide, and the marathon was a regular event until World War I. According to Syd Kronenthal, longtime Culver resident and former director of parks and recreation in Culver City, the next major marathon wouldn't come until the 1932 Olympic Marathon. A prime mover in that event was Paul Helms, the owner of Helms Bakeries, and since his bakery supplied foodstuffs for the 1932 Olympics, he was permitted to use the Olympic rings to advertise his "Helms Olympic Bread." In prior Olympics, all the teams fended for themselves, but in the 1932 Los Angeles Olympic Games, Olympic Villages were built to accommodate the athletes. One was constructed just beyond the city in the Baldwin Hills/Ladera area. But Paul Helms considered it a tragedy that the town didn't have its own marathon anymore, and he was ready to establish one. In 1948, Helms, Kronenthal and William Schroeder founded a marathon that would soon become the Western Hemisphere Marathon (WHM). The inaugural marathon followed the original Olympic route but was moved in 1949 to Culver City, where it became known as the Western Hemisphere Marathon. The marathon, which ran continuously until 2001, became the oldest marathon on the West Coast, second nationwide only to the Boston Marathon.

The Western Hemisphere Marathon celebrated several milestones. In 1951, it became the first marathon with a wheelchair division. From 1953 to 1955, city employee Bobby Cons (1949 winner) won an unprecedented three consecutive races and went on to qualify for the 1960 Olympic Marathon team. In 1956, the WHM qualified runners for Olympic team training. The 1964 WHM determined the United States' Olympic Marathon team for the games in Tokyo. The 1967 marathon was the first AAU-sanctioned race for women exceeding one mile (it was ten miles). In 1971, it was the first time women were welcomed to run along with men, and Patricia Bridges set the first AAU-sanctioned women's world record at 2:49:40. Steve Flynn tied local favorite Bobby Con's record of three consecutive victories for his performances in 1983–85. In 1991, the WHM was the final qualifying race for the 1992 Olympic Games in Barcelona, Spain. In 1995, the WHM was the final qualifying race for the Boston Marathon, and it introduced the first full marathon-length inline skating event in Los Angeles County. In 1997, the marathon celebrated its fiftieth anniversary. Other events have been added over the years, including a 5K and 10K run and a Walk for Education. The festivities always began and ended in front of the Veterans Memorial Auditorium. There is an impressive marker located where the start/finish lines cross Overland Avenue. The Western Hemisphere Marathon was generally scheduled for the first Sunday in December, drawing a diverse crowd including students, councilmembers and visitors from Kaizuka, our sister city in Japan.

In 1984, Culver City housed the Olympic Headquarters (currently the Costco site) and hosted two miles of the men's and first women's Olympic Marathon run through the city. The runners were greeted by Olympic

Culver City in the early days, looking north on Main Street. Early Culver City history was captured by an abundance of location filming in the downtown. Bank of America was on the left, and up the street, the saw indicated Steller Hardware.

banners along the route, which came into Culver City via the Marina Freeway and then went from Slauson Avenue, right onto Hannum, right onto Playa, right onto Overland and right onto Jefferson Boulevard, which led them back to the Coliseum.

Harry Culver was active in the community in its early years, serving as both a trustee and treasurer. As the city progressed, Culver moved his real estate office from the Story Building in Los Angeles to Culver City's Main Street, eventually relocating his large sales force to the Hotel Hunt (now the four-star Culver Hotel) after its construction was complete in 1924. A bronze public art piece depicting the Culver family can be seen in front of the Culver Hotel in downtown Culver City.

When Culver City was in its infancy, the Culver family lived on Delmas Terrace just north of Washington Boulevard. A detailed sketch of the home appeared in the October 31, 1914 edition of the *Culver City Call*. When the house became too small for the family and the area along Washington Boulevard started becoming commercial, Culver decided to build a mansion in nearby Cheviot Hills. About 1926, Culver split his Delmas Terrace house in half and moved it up to Cheviot Hills, where it was reassembled. He wanted to live in familiar surroundings while supervising the construction of his new mansion. The first home still exists on Club Drive in Cheviot Hills. It was renovated some years ago, and the Culver City Historical Society sponsored special tours of the home. According to the home's 1996 owners, the house was a three-story, 4,200-square-foot Colonial Revival structure. The architect remains unknown. There was significant earthquake damage in the 1994 Northridge quake that was repaired.

Patricia Culver Battle related that her father was impressed with the reputation and work of young architect Wallace Neff, who had designed Picfair Village and Cary Grant's home. Culver enlisted Neff to design the beautiful Culver mansion at 1845 Shelby Drive. Although Culver wanted an English-style home, according to his daughter, Neff suggested that he "consider Mediterranean Style, with lots of wrought iron." The Culver family enjoyed life in the Neff-designed mansion. One item of importance cited by Pat was that the new cook had to be able to make three things to please the city founder: "apple pie, soufflé, and beige bacon crisp."

PACIFIC MILITARY ACADEMY

It is a well-known fact that Harry H. Culver established the Pacific Military Academy (PMA) in honor of his father, Jacob Culver. A symbolic image of the PMA is a photo of Harry Culver on horseback on top of a hill. That photo was actually taken at the academy's second location, just north of Culver City.

The first Pacific Military Academy was built in the eastern portion of Culver City facing Washington Boulevard. A PMA publication dated 1923–24 offers a rare photo of the first school and tells of its beginnings:

> *The Pacific Military Academy was opened September 21st, 1922, in response to the demand for a boys' school situated in the country between Los Angeles and the sea, and carrying boys on from the lower grades through preparation for college or business. The academy has met with unqualified success in its work and has enjoyed a most gratifying increase in its enrolment.*

The publication notes that the academy was "situated at the eastern edge of Culver City, on Washington Boulevard, a short distance west of the Santa Monica Air Line tracks; less than ten minutes walk from the Post Office, stores and Pacific Electric Railway station." The board of directors was listed as "Harry H. Culver, President, Mrs. Katherine

Harry Culver's tribute to his father, Jacob Culver, was the Pacific Military Academy. This is the first location, on Culver City's Washington Boulevard in 1924. It later moved to Cheviot Hills. *Courtesy of Christina Machado Essex.*

Loughan, Managing Director, Hon. Benjamin F. Bledsoe, DeWitt Brady, B.C. Kelson, C.E. Lindblade and P.G. McDonnell." In a 1925 directory, the address of the PMA reads 6450 Washington Boulevard. According to the same directory, DeWitt Brady sold autos at 6420 Washington, and Lindblade, one of Culver's business associates, lived at 6500 Washington. Judge Bledsoe lived nearby on Club Drive.

In addition to a list of the articles of clothing needed by a cadet, there are also lists of administrative and academic staffs. The brochure lists Dr. F.M. Hull as the attending physician. The Hull Building, built by Dr. Hull in the 1920s, was the first hospital in town. It is one of the earliest sites marked by the Culver City Historical Society and later achieved city landmark status. Today it is home to Akasha, one of the city's new trendy restaurants.

One can also learn about the times by simply looking at the subject headings of the publication. The use of tobacco, for example, was prohibited and cause for dismissal. Bathing instructions, which would not have passed muster with many parents today, read, "Each cadet is required to take a shower bath at least twice a week and to change his underwear at the same time. Showers are the general rule after athletics. Tub baths can be had as required."

Historians search far and wide for accurate information. Robert Pennock, a Washington State resident, offers firsthand knowledge in the form of personal photos and a 1938 graduation program. The deckled-edge booklet is bound with blue cord and opens to a textured vellum cover with a formal Old English–style script that reads, "The Pacific Military Academy requests the honor of your presence during Senior Week, Culver City, California." The next pages list the members of the seventeen-cadet high school graduating class and items such as the senior class flower (white rose), senior class colors (royal purple and gold) and the senior class motto (*Sic Itur Ad Astra*). The program next lists the Pacific Order of the Military Cross (commander, knights, squires and pages) and the members of the fifteen-cadet junior school graduating class. This is followed by the staff page, which lists Lieutenant Colonel Harry H. Culver as president emeritus followed by Administrative Staff President Ensign Dominick Turinetto and others, including vice-president and headmaster, commandant of cadets, director of physical education, principal of junior school, secretary and registrar and nineteen faculty and staff officers. The medical staff consisted of two doctors, one a Dr. W.L. Mortensen, who was once Culver City's health officer, and a nurse.

A 1928 PMA publication showed H.H. Culver as the president, with Judge Benjamin F. Bledsoe serving as vice- president and Charles E. Lindblade as treasurer. (Note all three had streets in Culver City named for them.) The school ideals were listed as "high scholastic standards, physical development, military science and training for purposes of discipline, administration, uniformity and the development of leadership, moral character and training, responsibility of citizenship and Americanism." The publication also suggested that Harry Culver had been brought up with a "reverence for the traditions and customs of the military service."

The second Pacific Military Academy was a two-story structure designed by noted architect Wallace Neff, who had also designed the Culver family mansion nearby. The tuition in 1928 was listed as $800 a year for boarding or $200 for day attendance.

Mr. Charles Theodore Hill, who attended the Pacific Military Academy as a third and fourth grade cadet in 1939 and 1940, also shared information. When he attended PMA, there was a junior school, which was the equivalent of elementary school, and the upper classes, which started with seventh grade and continued through high school. There were generally two to a room, with the younger cadets living on the upper floor. Mr. Hill remembered each day beginning with "formation" when the flag was raised after a bugle call. Formation was held outdoors—weather permitting—and followed by the cadets marching to the mess hall. They ate at round tables, which all had big stainless steel or pewter pitchers of milk. Food was not an issue; there was plenty of it, according to Mr. Hill. After school, there was another formation, and after the lowering of the flag, the cadets marched to the mess hall for their evening meal.

Hill still has a school annual, *The Passing Parade*. He was especially glad it had a picture of the fallen radio tower, which he saw blow over, although no one believed him at the time. He remembered the school facing south at the top of a hill. Behind it was a horse-riding arena and a swimming pool. Hill said the academy was well organized and that it also had a golf team and rifle team.

On Saturday mornings, Mr. Hill said the boys had room inspection, after which they were free. Some went home, while others stayed. For weekend recreation, the boys took advantage of buses heading downtown, where some spent their twenty-five-cents-a-week allowance at the movies. At ten cents a movie, they could go to two movies at the Meralta and splurge on a five-cent candy bar!

The PMA functioned as a military school until World War II, when it housed combat photographers stationed at "Fort Roach" in Culver City. In a December 2000 interview at a combat photographers' reunion, Robert Elliott related that he had lived at the Pacific Military Academy for part of the time he was stationed at Fort Roach. Elliott arrived in 1943 when the PMA no longer appeared to be operating as a military school and worked on training films for the armed services. He had a corner room, which he found "adequate and within walking distance of the Hal Roach Studios and Downtown Culver City."

In 1946, the Wallace Neff–designed structure reopened as Cheviot Hills Military Academy. There was no address listed in the 1949 directory. The property's final days as a school began in 1952 as Chaminade, an all-boys' high school. This prime real estate was subdivided into a residential community in 1962.

CULVER'S LASTING INFLUENCE

The Culvers watched the city transformation until the Great Depression. Over time, Culver City has experienced peaks and valleys and has grown through forty annexations to nearly five square miles. Development preceded redevelopment, which could make history repeat itself. Harry Culver was right—it's all about location!

Harry Culver also donated the first acreage for Loyola University. He and Fritz Burns felt that a university in the vicinity of the community would enhance its economic viability. Culver received an honorary doctorate from nearby Loyola University in 1930. The school is still flourishing today as Loyola-Marymount University.

Above: Culver City established an Art in Public Places ordinance in 1988, followed by a Historic Preservation ordinance in 1991. *A Moment in Time*, a bronze sculpture by De L'Espric, serves both goals in depicting Harry Culver's family in 1917, the year the city was incorporated. Culver's grandson, John Battle, and his family posed in front of the Culver Hotel during a visit to the city.

Opposite: One of Culver's early ads picturing his Delmas Terrace home at the top. The intended balanced community is obvious from the emphasis on "Home City" and commerce with "All Roads Lead to Culver City."

Culver eventually traded the Neff mansion for a penthouse at the Sunset Towers in Los Angeles. The Neff mansion is pictured in books on the famous architect. By the time Harry Culver moved to the Sunset Towers, he was no longer active in Culver City. Culver died at the age of 66 in a Hollywood hospital in 1946 after a number of strokes. Mrs. Culver passed away in 1999 at 103. Pat Culver Battle, their daughter, continued to support city events until her own death in 2001. Her sons and grandchildren remain helpful supporters of the Culver City Historical Society.

When Harry Culver announced his plan for Culver City in 1913, he had diligently researched this area, the climate and other factors that would

Today there are 7 miles of paved streets and cement sidewalks; an extensive and substantial business and industrial district; many attractive homes and a beautiful little city park and electric fountain—where just a few months ago was an expanse of empty acreage.

Where all Home-Building records are being smashed. As sure as the electric magnet draws particles of steel —Culver City is attracting home-builders and home lovers from all sections of Southern California.

A great reailway manager said recently, "Culver City has a WONDERFUL LOCATION—that asset alone will make it a leading city."

The growth of Culver City in 10 months is the most remarkable suburban estate development of 1914.

Culver City will surprise you, captivate you, convince you. You've seen what has happened at Hollywood, Pasadena, Long Beach and Venice. Culver City's "next!" See this new wondertown and your good judgment will do the rest.

If you should sit on the shady veranda of a Culver City home—could sense the fresh tonic ocean air, see the delicate color-shades of the distant mountains and feel the comfortable, uncrowded, homey atmosphere of the place—you wouldn't wonder at Culver City's wonderful record of growth and development. Culver City has suburban transportation facilities unequaled on the Pacific Coast.

All Roads Lead to Culver City

DEL REY LINE
WASHINGTON BLVD
VENICE SHORT LINE
PICO BLVD
PUTNAM BLVD
AIR LINE
NAT'L SILV

...the home city

HarryH.Culver Co.
ACREAGE
VENICE — LOS ANGELES
Second Floor Hollingsworth Bldg.
Home 60632   Sixth and Hill   Main 8045
BRANCH OFFICE—CULVER CITY

Culver City is served by Four Big Boulevards and Three Great Interurban Electric Lines— 159 cars a day, a Motor Bus every 15 minutes lead to a successful city. In his speech at the California Club in downtown Los Angeles, Culver shared his vision with his colleagues. He spoke of California's draw and cited the development of the City of Los Angeles and Abbot Kinney's resort of Venice of America.

Harry Culver proposed a family-oriented, balanced community with an economic base to support it. He ensured that by the city's proximity to transportation routes. In his early ad in the *Culver City Call*, he called Culver City the "home city." The ad suggested that the city would become a magnet for homebuilders, falling right in line with other successful developments such as Hollywood, Pasadena, Long Beach and Venice. He referred to Culver City as a "wondertown." In the fine print, the ad stated, "If you should sit on the shady veranda of a Culver City home, you could sense the fresh tonic ocean air, see the delicate shades of the distant mountains and feel the comfortable, uncrowded homey atmosphere of the place."

And so in 1913, after Culver had filed his little Main Street with the county, development began to flourish. Culver and his partners transformed parts of two old Spanish ranchos, Rancho La Ballona and Rancho Rincón de los Bueyes, into a viable community. He enticed movie studios to his city as a part of the economic base, and an early annexation guaranteed miles of Washington Boulevard's commercial benefits. People were driving from the big city to Venice along that route. And just as he predicted, the big city would grow toward Culver City, which in turn would grow toward Los Angeles.

CULVER CITY GOVERNMENT

There seems to be great interest in the early elected officials who served Culver City. The photo on the following page was taken in 1920 when the officials were meeting at their first location, the current site of the Culver Hotel. City Resolution #4 authorized the city "to lease from Fannie A. Henderson, the upper floor—without the projection room" as "suitable quarters for carrying on business in a building known as Culver Theatre." The cost of the upstairs room was fifteen dollars per month. The decision was 5-0. The board of trustees met there until 1922, when it moved down the street to 415–17 Van Buren Place at the request of Harry Culver, who planned to build the Hotel Hunt (now the Culver Hotel) on the location.

1920 city officials. *Left to right*: Charles E. Shillito, city treasurer; Reve Houck, trustee; Daniel F. Coombs, mayor; John Imil, city attorney; Clyde W. Slater, trustee; Nellie Haus, city clerk; Milton Gardener, trustee; and Clarence Loop, trustee. *Courtesy of the Coombs family.*

The city trustees later became known as city council members, and from the early days, there was an elected city clerk and city treasurer. Culver City became a charter city in 1947. In a 2006 charter revision, the chief administrative officer form of government was replaced by a city manager form of government, and the previously elected city clerk and treasurer became appointed positions.

Since Culver City's September 20, 1917 incorporation, the city clerk's office shows the following as Culver City trustees and council members as of 2013: R.P. Davidson, Walter Edwards, B.J. Higuera, V.R. Day, Belle Wyant Day, Dan F. Coombs, Harry H. Culver, Clyde Slater, W.S. McNeir, Clarence V. Loop, Reve E. Houck, Earl Bobier, David E. Clark, H.W. Kinkead, Michael Tellefson, John F. Lehman, Philip M. Stephon, Guy E. Heaton, Arthur Segrell, R.H. Segrell, Francis Robert Reeves, Adin A. Randall, Ray L. Haskell, J. Ray Klots, Walter H. Hahn, Robert C. Lacomb, Curtis J. Davis, Thomas J. Carroll, William G. Douglas Jr., Leroy Koos, Edward T.

Castle, Harlan J. Thompson, Joseph L. Sullivan, Ed Juline, Harold J. Shields, Duke P. Watson, James C. Roberts, Mary Lou Richardson, Robert Unruhe, Raymond O'Neal, Garland F. Garrett, G. William Botts, Daniel Patacchia, Gerald A. Margolis, Joe Lawless, James Astle Jr., Ed Little, Martin A. Lotz, John Carl Brogdon, Richard Pachtman, Dr. James Boulgarides, Richard Alexander, A. Ronald Perkins, Richard Ross Brundo, Paul Jacobs, Paul A. Netzel, Jozelle Smith, Steven Gourley, Ian Michael Balkman, Albert Vera, Edward Wolkowitz, Sandra Levin, Richard Marcus, David Hauptman, Alan Corlin, Carol Gross, Steven J. Rose, Gary Silbiger, Scott Malsin, Christopher Armenta, Micheal O'Leary, Andrew Weissman, Jeffrey Cooper, Meghan Sahli-Wells and Jim Clarke.

CITY HALLS

A "City Hall Fund" was created by Resolution #334 on July 30, 1923, by the Culver City Board of Trustees. This action was intended to provide the necessary funds for "the acquisition, erection and equipping of an adequate city hall." In 1923, the city offices were located on Van Buren, just south of Washington Boulevard. They had been moved out of the second floor of the theater building in 1922 so that Harry Culver could begin construction on his hotel. The following year, the council recognized that public interest and necessity demanded that the new city hall house the city offices, police headquarters and a central fire station (Resolution #418, February 25, 1924). In 1925, the trustees provided for bonds to finance the new city structures.

As time passed, the plans became more definitive. By 1927, the fire station was planned to be a stand-alone building just east of the new city hall. The contract for the station was awarded to Byerts and Dunn, "the lowest responsible bidders," on October 17, 1927. Two months later, the trustees rejected all bids for the new city hall. Trustees Coombs and Bobier were appointed as a committee to advise and work with the architect in preparation and submission of plans to bring cost down to $100,000.

On January 3, the bids were opened for city hall. Architect Orville Clark noted that the bids ranged from $95,000 to $120,000, with R.P. Davidson's bid being the lowest. Interestingly, Davidson had served earlier as the first building inspector in Culver City. So in 1928, the city hall was built, and in 1929, Culver City dedicated its first structure specifically built to house

The city offices were moved from the second floor of the early theater to Van Buren so that Harry Culver could build his "skyscraper" hotel. The police and fire departments enjoyed their first spaces at this location. The Baldwin Hills appear in the background.

The first structure to be built as a city hall opened in 1929. It is pictured here in the 1950s. Some of the architectural elements were saved and can be found along the Culver Boulevard bike path. The building was also memorialized in films such as *County Hospital* (Laurel and Hardy) and the *Hunter* TV show.

The new city hall opened in 1995 with a façade entry reminiscent of the 1928 city hall, which had occupied the same site. It was marked as Historic Site #1, and at the corner, there is a new plaque and directional sign to celebrate sister city relationships.

city offices. The building was situated on the corner of Culver (previously Putnam Avenue) and Duquesne. Culver City's current city hall was opened in June 1995 on the same site. During construction, the city offices were moved to the northwest corner of Overland Avenue and Culver Boulevard, where the Senior Center is located today. When you walk through the entry to city hall, you should be aware that the freestanding structure is a three-fourths replica of the 1928 city hall. It was designed to look like a movie set façade—an important symbol of the movie industry that makes Culver City the "Heart of Screenland." There are plaques on either side of the entrance, the original one celebrating the opening of the 1928 city hall and the other commemorating the current structure.

CULVER CITY POLICE DEPARTMENT

In a letter dated February 25, 1914, from Venice, F.J. Barton, constable of the Ballona Township of Los Angeles County, advised Harry Culver that he had appointed F.C. Cole as chief of police. The letter was in response to a phone call the day before about the "policing of Culver City."

In 1917, the year the city was incorporated, the city trustees, in their fifth resolution, provided for the appointment of a city marshal. Frank W. Bradley was to serve the city beginning November 21 for $25 a month. The city also adopted a resolution to use the county jail for prisoners and appointed a committee of three (with full power) to arrange for police protection of the city utilizing the sheriff's department. The board of trustees authorized appointment of temporary police officers as the need arose. Five more marshals were appointed through 1926, beginning with E.G. Mason, who also served as the ex officio tax and license collector at $25 a month. Appointed after Mason was M. Sprankling, who served for five years and also held the office of "Night Police," followed by W. Smith and J. Cain. Walter Shaw became the first municipal chief of police in 1926. In those early years, policing was very different. In 1920, for example, the trustees discontinued all motor officers because the legal department of the Automobile Club advised that it was just a matter of time until all municipalities would have to remit all fines on public highways to the county treasurer. Culver City was simply "unable to expend $300 a month for motorcycle officers."

By 1922, police-enforced rules included, "No dancing in Cafes and Restaurants after 11 p.m." Two years later, the needs of the city demanded the acquisition of property for a city hall and a police headquarters. On December 15, 1924, the trustees took action to acquire three steel cells for the police department, and the police were commended for efficiently handling the crowds on opening day of the Speedway Racetrack. Duties were expanded in 1927, as U. Barnett became the first school-crossing officer. Cecil B. DeMille was given a badge and appointed as a special police officer in 1927. The following year, police were faced with enforcing the trustees' unanimous decision to prohibit the "shaking of dice for money, merchandise or credit and certain games."

In 1929, the police were sent to Fatty Arbuckle's Plantation Cafe to summon the owners to appear at their next meeting. The same day, action was taken to refuse a license to the "gypsies" operating a business at 7024 Washington Boulevard. The police received additional responsibilities when the Culver City Kennel Club received a five-year permit for canine racing. In those years, the city was notorious for its nightclubs, bookies and gambling. The irregular city boundaries added to enforcement nightmares, and there were a few "tarnished badges" to be dealt with as well. Policing included location shooting in the city and the protection of movie stars

In the 1940s, Culver City's finest were located in the westerly portion of the 1928 city hall. This is where the *Nightwatch* radio and TV programs began.

such as the "little people" who arrived for the filming of *The Wizard of Oz* starting in 1938.

In early times, the average tenure of office for a chief was two years. Following Walter Shaw were Chiefs Costigan, Daudel, Hendry (who left to become a studio police chief), Smith, Weatherly, Miller, Truschel, McDonald, Carnahan, Postal, Muchmore, Arkoff, Olsen, Hildebrand, Mueller, Mennig and Walter. Chief Ted Cooke served from 1976 to 2003 and was followed by Interim Chief Gary Martin, Chief John Montanio and Interim Chief Bill Burck. Chief Don Pedersen has served from 2006 to the present.

The police station has had a Duquesne address since the 1920s, first at the side of city hall and then in its own building. The current station was expanded and rededicated in 1999. Change was the norm as the city grew from 1.2 to almost 5 square miles. There was a mounted reserve posse established in 1948, which was followed by Culver City officers starring in *Nightwatch*, the first police reality radio and TV show.

Culver City police officers who once had to watch the Veterans Memorial Tower beacon for a summons to work are now at the forefront of technology, individually equipped with digitally coded secure equipment and aided by camera traffic enforcement. Today, sworn police officers number 106 and probably hold the highest percentage of advanced degrees in the state. CCPD competes for grant funding, utilizes asset seizure funds and canines and has encouraged many prevention programs, including Juvenile Diversion, DARE, Reserves and Neighborhood Watch.

Nightwatch

Culver City is often on the cutting edge, and when it comes to reality shows, the city's participation actually began during the radio era. *Nightwatch* was the brainchild of police reporter Donn Reed. It was a "ride-along" program during which the reporter wore a hidden microphone and rode along with a Culver City police unit at night. A constant from the department was Officer Ron Perkins, who also served as the show's technical advisor.

Nightwatch was born in the 1950s, when entry to the police headquarters was located on Duquesne in the old city hall. Hildebrand was police chief at the time, and Perkins was a sergeant. The show's announcer always began with the following disclaimer: "The sounds you are hearing are real. Remember, all the people you hear are not actors. All voices and sounds are authentic." Each episode followed the action during the night watch—6:00 p.m. to 2:00 a.m.—and programs ended with a narrative wrap-up from the chief.

The show was such a hit that Perkins and Reed transitioned it to television. Most thought it would be too complicated, especially the idea of filming at night. Bill Burrud, who had produced *Wanderlust* and *Vagabond*, was the only one up to the challenge. Bill Burrud Productions picked up *Nightwatch* for KCOP TV on Wednesday nights. At the time, Burrud said, "This is more than just a drama—this is life itself. This is *Nightwatch*." Donn Reed and our own Ron Perkins became a television team, working together as "Detective Unit FIVE SIX" with the cooperation of new chief Eugene Mueller, who enjoyed a certain amount of drama.

Ron Perkins retired from the CCPD as a captain. He then served as a council member in Culver City, and after he and his wife, Barbara (also a Culver City police officer), moved to the desert, Ron served on La Quinta's city council. The last time I spoke with Ron, he told me that a Perkins had served on the CCPD in each of the last fifty years. His son must have the tradition up to fifty-five years by now.

The radio version of *Nightwatch* can be accessed online at Old Time Radio Fan (www.otrfan.com/). There are a few of the twenty-minute shows available, in which you can hear the familiar voices of then-young Ron Perkins, Sergeant Bob Conlon, Lieutenant Charles Lugo and others.

CULVER CITY FIRE DEPARTMENT

The histories of our city's fire department and the studios' fire departments overlap in early years. In the city records, one might find first mention of the Culver City Fire Department (CCFD) as City Resolution #50, adopted in 1919 when Manuel "Sy" Saenz was appointed as fire chief for ten dollars per month. The firetruck was kept at Saenz's garage at Washington and Ince. According to a 1947 *Evening Star News* interview with Arthur G. Withrow, one of the few living original firemen, Saenz recruited volunteers as needed on the way to the fire. Volunteers were paid one dollar for false alarms, three dollars for chemical fires and four dollars for a fire during which a hose was used. Legend has it that so much junk was in the way of the truck that the firemen were often late to fires—including the fire in which Mayor Clyde Slater's garage burned down.

The firetruck was later moved from the Saenz garage to Earl Bobier's garage at Washington and Irving Place. During these early times, L.B. Minnick, the fire chief at the Thomas H. Ince Studios (now Culver Studios), was appointed as acting chief. According to Withrow, "It was on October 6, 1922, that the first organized fire department blessed the taxpayers of Culver City." Frank Wilcox became fire chief and recruited volunteers, including Withrow, who worked for the city; Jack Burns, the head mechanic at the Hal Roach Studios; and Harry D'Arcey and Seeley R. Barton, also Roach employees. Early stories like the firetruck running out of gas and the hose sending the mayor's hat into the flames were material for comedies.

Ray Moselle worked for the Culver City Fire Department from 1937 to 1972. He has fond memories of his time in the department, which dates back to when there were only two shifts, with four firemen at Station #1 and two firemen at Station #2. MGM had its own separate six-man fire department. At one time, the MGM Studios fire department was larger than the city's. MGM had an old United firetruck, a one-thousand-gallon pumper that later went to the city as a reserve rig. Some studio firemen, like Gordon "Doc" Donovan, worked for MGM first and went on to work for CCFD. Moselle related that many local firemen welcomed the opportunity to work standby jobs for filming during their time off. He remembered working on Orson Welles's *Citizen Kane* and recalled that they had to turn off the fire sprinklers on the stage during filming—not a comfortable situation for any firefighter. Moselle noted that all the off-duty firemen worked on *Gone with the Wind* in the scene where they "burned Atlanta" on the backlot at Selznick. He also

The Culver City Fire Department was built next door to the 1928 city hall on Culver Boulevard.

worked on the first *Mutiny on the Bounty* film with Charles Laughton in the scene where they "rocked the boat in a tank."

One of the most remembered studio fires occurred in 1925, when a fire on a DeMille Studios (now Culver Studios) stage spread to the paint shop, carpenter shop and another stage. Culver City was joined by Los Angeles units, and together they battled the blaze for sixteen hours. Another frightening studio fire took place at MGM when the sets from *The Good Earth* went up in flames in one of the scene docks. MGM's fire department was phased out by the early 1960s. Sony Pictures, which took over the old MGM Lot #1 in 1990, still has a firetruck, although it relies on the Culver City Fire Department regularly and recruits off-duty CCFD firemen while filming.

By 1927, the construction of Fire Station #1 was underway, as was that of the new city hall at Culver and Duquesne. That same year, after annexation of the west end, Station #2 was located in a house on McConnell Boulevard. It was a gift of the water company, which saw that the area was underserved. Station #2 was relocated to Washington Boulevard in 1981. Station #1 was relocated a block west of its original location and reopened in 1993. The third station, which was built at Berryman and Segrell in 1956, was replaced by a new one in Fox Hills in 2009. Culver City Fire Department has been known as a Class 1 fire department since 1995. Known for its fast response times and fine paramedic services, Culver City proudly touts the CCFD as one of the advantages of living in the city, and local families flock to the fire stations for their annual Fire Service Day in May. Many locals also volunteer for the Community Emergency Response Team (CERT) program. Fire chiefs over the years have reached out to the community, and some of the chiefs you might remember include John Kearney, Burt Campbell, George Sweeny, Mike Thompson, Mike Olson and Jeff Eastman. Today, Christopher Sellers heads this extraordinary city department.

CULVER CITY BUS DEPARTMENT

While Harry Culver's first ads boasted that "all roads lead to Culver City," further reading disclosed that Culver City was served by "four big boulevards and three great interurban electric lines." A decade later, in the late 1920s, the *Evening Star News* pointed out a drawback in the system in the "burdensome rates charged by the Pacific Electric." That same newspaper enthusiastically reported that Mayor Reve Houck had announced that the city, under a provision of the state constitution, could operate its own transportation service. Mayor Houck and the board of trustees, recognizing the need for inexpensive public transportation, went to work to make it happen. According to Houck's daughter, Alene Houck Johnson, Mayor Houck was very concerned that the rented buses might be sabotaged. Legend has it that Houck financed the first bus. Bus transportation was enthusiastically supported by the community, which voted for a bond to finance the second oldest municipal bus line in the state.

As of March 3, 2008, Culver City had provided eighty years of continuous bus service to its citizens, and to celebrate its anniversary, the city offered "Culver CityBus Free Fare Day." Today, Culver City buses board approximately 5.8 million passengers each year for safe rides on their fleet of compressed natural gas (CNG) buses.

MGM's Landmark Colonnade in the late 1920s serves as the background for a celebration of Culver City's new municipal bus line, the second in the state.

In 2012, the 100 Best Fleets National Fleet Certification/Recognition Program named Culver City the third best municipal fleet in North America out of thirty-eight thousand public fleets.

And why is the Culver CityBus logo so recognizable? The fonts/script came from the lettering on the neon tower and marquee of the landmark 1947 Culver Theatre.

CITY STREETS

Streets are named when tract maps are filed with the county. In early times, street names often reflected developers' families and colleagues, as well as local history.

Machado Road cut through the former Studio Drive-In property. The 1994 dedication included Machado family genealogist Fred Machado (right) and cousin Michael Machado and his wife, Angie, and daughter Jasmine.

The first tract, #1775, was filed in 1912 by Camillo Cereghino and his Washington Boulevard Improvement Co. Many of those streets were named for international and national figures, like presidents: (George) Washington, (Abraham) Lincoln, (James) Madison, (Martin) Van Buren and (Andrew) Jackson. Other streets were named after Abraham Duquesne, a French naval officer; British commander Edward Braddock; Civil War naval commander Admiral David Farragut; La Salle, a French explorer; and the Marquis de Lafayette, a French statesman/general who served in the Continental army during the American Revolution.

Tract #2444, filed on September 11, 1913, by the Culver Investment Co., included Main Street and land north to Pico (which was outside Culver City). Tract #2530 was a Higuera filing, which explains the 1919 naming of Higuera Street. The Higueras founded Rancho Rincón de los Bueyes, which was the second rancho from which Culver City was carved (there was no Rancho Higuera).

In some instances, street names were changed to be consistent with the county master street plan. A street name in Culver City, for example, was often changed for continuity with its Los Angeles extension. In 1950, Bankfield Avenue was changed to Hayter Avenue by ordinance CS-130 "to reduce confusion and serve the public interest." Likewise, Moynier Lane was changed to South Fairfax and La Cienega.

In later times, the history of MGM's Lot #3 yielded names like Raintree, Bounty Lane and St. Louis Street, which celebrated movies filmed on that land. Studio Estates was part of another movie backlot, MGM's Lot #2. Developer Goldrich & Kest named streets for MGM stars like Fred Astaire, Jackie Coogan and Judy Garland.

Culver Crest immortalized developer Lou Crank's wife, Esther, with Esterina Way. Lugo Way was named for the Californio (1774) family of Charles Lugo. Stephon Terrace was named for 1930s councilman and police commissioner Phillip Stephon, while Tellefson Road was named for city official Mike Tellefson. Stubbs Lane, a private road, led to former city clerk Helene Stubbs's home. Youngworth was named for the early developer/attorney Leo Youngworth, whose historic home is marked on the Marycrest Manor property.

Blair Hills developers Stone & Stone came up with Stoneview, Vicstone and Blairstone Streets. Early area residents Lois Soter and Mim Shapiro have verified that Blair was the name of a Stone grandchild. Blanco Way refers to R.J. Blanco, who developed Studio Village, while Coombs Avenue honors early city trustee and contractor Dan Coombs.

Cota Street references an early family and relatives of the Machado family. Hacienda Street was changed in 1949 to Culver Center Street. Putnam Avenue was renamed Culver Boulevard in 1926, while another portion was changed from Del Rey Boulevard in 1927.

Delmas Terrace refers to Harry Culver's business partner Delphin Delmas. Dobson Way was a 1950 name change from Whitehead Street to honor Mayor Frank Dobson. Segrell Way honors former mayor A.H. Segrell.

Eastham Drive was named for Earl Eastham, a business associate and brother-in-law of Harry Culver. Lindblade was another of Culver's associates and the developer of the landmark Washington Building.

Overland Avenue has been First Street, Flower Street and, originally, the "Road to San Pedro." The port of San Pedro was important to early settlers and traders like Agustín Machado. Steller was named for the Main Street hardware store owner Adolph Steller (Steller and Skoog), the chamber president who actively promoted the Hayden Tract in the 1940s.

Hazelton, aka "Fear Street," was renamed Kinston to project a better image, while Elenda Street was named for the wife of John D. Young, who acquired a Talamantes portion of Rancho La Ballona.

Hayden was the developer of the first industrial tract in Culver City, and Helms Avenue edges the Helms Bakery Building. Ince Boulevard commemorates Thomas Ince, who built the first two major studios in Culver City.

Jefferson Boulevard was changed from Machado in 1925. In 1994, the new connector between Jefferson and Sepulveda was named Machado Road to honor the early settler family. Nearby Agustín Street bears the first name of the Machado who founded Rancho La Ballona. Ballona, of course, was named for the Machado/Talamantes rancho. Lantana, in the Heritage Park development, was named for the city flower, while Heritage Place honors the diverse heritage of Culver City residents.

And for those of us who have been here awhile, you might remember that we almost had a Rocky Road—not for the ice cream but for the *Rocky* movies!

PARKS

Media Park, adjacent to the Ivy Substation, was named by a pharmacist from Palms. City founder Harry Culver offered a trip around the world to the winning entry in his contest to name the park. Technically located in Los Angeles, it has been on a long-term lease from the city, along with the Ivy Substation, since 1987.

Dr. Paul Carlson Park was originally Victory Park (on property dedicated by the Speedway subdividers in 1927) but renamed for the young medical missionary, who was born in Culver City in 1928 and died in the Congo in the 1960s. The park's original name was long thought to be associated with the United States' victory in World War I. But according to Alene Houck Johnson, there is evidence to substantiate that the wife of Mayor Reve Houck offered the name Victory Park because "it was a victory to have a park in Culver City."

Lindberg Park began as two acres dedicated by the Title and Guarantee Trust Co. and accepted by the city in 1927. The city received six additional lots at no cost, extending the park to Cota Street in 1938. The park's name remains in question. Early city records show an "h" at the end of the word, and since Charles Lindbergh did visit Culver City and had a relationship with city founder Harry Culver, it could have been named for the famed aviator. There were also local Lindberghs listed in early directories. One can only hope that time will unearth the real answer!

Culver West Alexander Park, formerly West End Park, was named for the area of the city in which it is located. That area was an early annexation to the city in the mid-1920s, although it still carries a different zip code. It was

The first park in Culver City was Victory Park. The property was first used in the 1920s as a horse-racing track and then as the famed Speedway before it became Victory Park in 1927. It was renamed for medical missionary Dr. Paul Carlson in the 1960s.

renamed to honor the memory of former mayor and city council member Richard Alexander, who also served on the parks and recreation commission.

Syd Kronenthal Park, formerly McManus Park, was renamed for our (now retired) legendary director of parks and recreation, Sydney Kronenthal. It is situated at the east end of the city at the foot of McManus Street, which was named by Los Angeles prior to its annexation to Culver City. Both Syd Kronenthal and Mike Tellefson proactively promoted park space in Culver City.

Veterans Memorial Park, renamed in 1949, began as Exposition Park when the first land was acquired in 1938. Many veterans' organizations are commemorated on the entry walls of the 1950 Veterans Memorial Building at the edge of the park. According to a July 1938 newspaper clipping, the original plans called for a "studio park" at the corner of Overland and Culver Boulevard with a "180 foot tower, beautifully lighted, and with fountains playing on the outside. Stairs inside will allow visitors to climb to the lookouts which overlook the entire studio area." There was also the promise of a small lake in the park. A corporation was formed, with Eugene Donovan, owner/publisher of the *Citizen* newspaper, taking the president's seat of a board that included Mayor Arthur Segrell; P.M. Stephon, councilman; A.M. Campbell, school board chairman; William Shea, editor of the *Culver City Star*; Colonel William Evans, chair emeritus of the chamber of commerce; Frank Whitbeck, an MGM vice-president; and Blaine Walker, then president of the Culver City Chamber of Commerce. The corporate attorney was Mike Tellefson, who was also the city attorney.

The city purchased the first acreage from the Security First National Bank on January 10, 1938. The intent was to complete this project in April 1939 as Exposition Park. However, the acreage was increased to 10.95 acres, and the park was renamed Veterans Memorial Park in August 1949. At the time, the site excluded the library building, which became the Senior Citizens Center in 1972 and most recently was refurbished to accommodate a new Teen Center. This was the largest park until the city acquired the 40.0-acre Culver City Park.

The Veterans Memorial Building cornerstone was laid in 1950. The building opened with a 122-foot tower, and as per the original plans, the Rotunda Room was designated as a museum. The well-attended dedication included Lieutenant Governor Goodwin J. Knight, along with the guests of honor, the Gold Star Mothers. Entertainment was provided by the movie industry, according to an article in the *Citizen*. It also reported that the swimming pool (Plunge) had been recently completed.

Today, the Veterans Memorial Building honors those who fought for our freedom with many plaques in the entry. The park has hosted many celebrations, including the local Fiesta La Ballona. The building has been refurbished more than once. Within the building, there are rooms named for each of our sister cities. After the 1980 "re-do," artist Natalie Kroll was commissioned to design *Filmstrip USA*, which was unveiled in 1981 with the help of actress Linda Gray, who grew up in Culver City. A recent change is the conversion of a portion of the building to an archival space. It is not the promised movie museum, but as the Culver City Historical Society Archives and Resource Center, it offers full access to the rich history of the area. The Veterans Memorial Building was marked as Historic Site No. 13 by the Culver City Historical Society in December 2011. The bronze plaque is visible at the front of the building.

Huell Howser's 2010 visit to Culver City elicited a lot of questions, as many were reminded of the "Tower" and the "Tower Restaurant," which was located inside the Veterans Memorial Building on the site of the current Lethbridge Garden Room. It was often pictured with its long canopy/

The Veterans Memorial Building was built in 1950 as a community space at the edge of Veterans Memorial Park. The tower offered a view from the ocean to downtown Los Angeles, but locals were mostly interested in the view into the studio lots across Culver Boulevard.

awning, which stretched from the sidewalk to the building entrance. On the Culver Boulevard side, there was a pole sign advertising the restaurant.

When the Veterans Memorial Building was constructed in 1950 via a $550,000 bond, the original plans called for a "recreational building with a stage, restaurant, film museum, playroom, and large gymnasium." The city leased out the restaurant space first to Louis and Marion Migler, who called it Marion's Tower Restaurant. That was the way it was listed in the 1959–60 local telephone directory. Marion moved to "Downtown Culver City" and established Marion's Party Center on the east side of the street, which, to be accurate, was actually Bagley Avenue in Los Angeles. Ray Rappoport later took over the Tower Restaurant, and one of his employees, Dorothy Kinnon, became the last owner. Dorothy, a local favorite, kept the restaurant open about a year before transitioning it into Tower Caterers. Former city treasurer Lu Herrera shared that, at one time, the chamber of commerce used the Rotunda Room for its breakfast meetings, which benefitted from the use of Tower Catering. Organizations like the Soroptimist Club later met in the room where the restaurant once existed.

Doneil Kinnon Weissman, who helped her mother at the restaurant at times, remembered the Tower Restaurant as a dark place with booths, some arranged around the columns, which are still in the room. She recalled that it was generally open for lunch and special occasions. Her fond memories include riding the elevator up to the top of the tower to "see all of Culver City." The restored Winchester Chimes were a gift of the Culver City Rotary Club.

To update its history, the restaurant later became the Garden Room, and in 1980, when the Veterans Memorial Building was renovated the first time, the west wall became mostly windows, opening the room into the patio. The wall adjacent to the windows was rounded for a mural, with the goal being to open it up further. The idea was to increase its use for parties and receptions. Syd Kronenthal, then director of human services, asked that the mural have a landscape format with "backlot movie set" references.

Blanco Park carries the name of Ray Blanco, the developer of the lower hill area and Blanco Way. Blanco donated the land in 1951 for the use of a park in perpetuity.

El Marino Park was established on land purchased in 1954 by the city from Washington Improvement Co. developer Camillo Cereghino and his wife, Marie. It was originally known as Culver Park.

Tellefson Park, formerly the Rollerdrome skating rink, was dedicated during the 1976 bicentennial. It was named for Mike Tellefson, who served the city in a variety of capacities, including council member and city attorney, for thirty-one years.

Bill Botts Field in Culver City Park is the site of our Little League/soccer fields. It was named for 1960s two-term council member Bill Botts, who fought for the space for the Little League fields. The park, annexed from the county in 1982, boasts forty acres and is the largest city park to date. There is a family park at the base of the hill, and on the way up, a walking track is apparent, just before you see the Culver City Dog Park.

Coombs Park was named for a prominent local family. Dan Coombs was an early city trustee and local contractor who built many homes, as well as Fatty Arbuckle's Plantation Cafe. The Coombs family still has a presence in the city.

Fox Hills Park was named for the Fox Hills area, a 1964 annexation to Culver City. This eleven-acre park was part of the first major Culver City Redevelopment project.

Heritage Park is located on the former site of the Studio Drive-In. The developer of the area, the Lee Group/Braemar Urban Ventures, named it to honor everyone's heritage.

ANNEXATIONS

Culver City's boundaries are so irregular because the city is a product of a plethora of annexations. The first land tract was filed with Los Angeles County on September 17, 1917, and amounted to 770 acres, or 1.2 square miles. As development occurred, each new area was annexed. Perhaps the best illustration is a map from the Culver City Engineering Department, which can be accessed on the city website: www.culvercity.org.

We can be relatively sure that economics played a big part in most annexations, particularly on #6, known as the Walnut Annexation. Was it added for the commercial strip leading to Venice or the racetrack at Walnut and Washington? The Depression took its toll, and the city boundary did not change again until 1943. There were three more annexations in the 1940s, followed by sixteen in the 1950s, including a detachment to Palms. Twelve actions took place in the 1960s, with one each in the next three decades. As of this writing, Culver City, through forty-one actions, boasts a net size of 4.954 square miles.

It is generally an exciting time when the circus comes to town. Did you know that Culver City land was used by a circus in the 1920s? Walnut Park was one of the largest single additions to the city, encompassing 484 acres, or about three-fourths of a square mile. It spanned from Venice Boulevard down to Havelock, but the most remarkable part of the annexation was the long slender piece extending to Walnut (the street before Lincoln Boulevard), which at one point is just three hundred feet across. Over the years, there have been several landmark businesses in that area. At Berryman, the Al

G. Barnes Circus used that land as its winter quarters after returning from its travels around the country. Many residents in the area have found rings used to tie the animals buried in their backyards. Some even remember the elephants! In 2002, cousins Fred and Pat Machado pinpointed the circus headquarters as being situated between Washington and Culver Boulevards at Berryman. Pat said it faced Washington. Early on, the circus was located in an area known as Barnes City. Although it had a council and a city hall at Centinela and Louise (which became Centinela Feed), it was legally in question and dissolved in 1927.

"Venice Joe" Lescoulie (cousin to our "Culver City" Joe Lescoulie) recalled that same year that the "circus was housed in regular buildings, like a permanent camp." He had vivid recollections of hearing the lions roar, all the way to the Lescoulie Dairy on Glencoe (Ocean Park Avenue at that time). He remembered that the animals were brought in "on the rails down by Culver Boulevard for the Winter Quarters. Some stayed all year—perhaps they were sick or too old." The sign on the front of the building declared it the "Winter Home of the Al G. Barnes Circus." The owner's full name was Alpheus George Barnes Stonehouse. Barnes billed his circus as the home of Tusko, the largest elephant in the world, and Lotus, the largest hippopotamus in the world. According to signage on the structure, it operated as a zoo, with daily hours from 10:00 a.m. to 11:00 p.m. Its monkeys, opossum and baby elk were also part of its advertised draw. The circus, in which local resident Ben Pitti performed his rope and knife-throwing tricks, eventually folded into the American Circus Corp., which then became a part of the Ringling Brothers Circus.

Blair Hills was carved from a portion of Rancho Rincón de los Bueyes, owned by the Higuera family. It was a part of the Baldwin Hills and was rich with oil fields. According to official city records, it was added in 1921 as Annexation #2, the Smith annexation. By the early 1950s, the property had already developed a colorful history. La Cienega was not yet a street, and the area close to Kenneth Hahn Park had been used as an Olympic Village in 1932. The major property owners were the Schultz family, Charlie Wright (Wrightcrest Drive), Hetzler, Moynier (Moynier Lane) and Will Rogers Jr.

A shy Will Rogers Jr. was raised on his actor father's Santa Monica ranch, played his father in movies, served in Congress and worked in the newspaper business. Will Rogers's chauffeur had been a talented performer by the name of Ben Pitti (stage name Bennie Pete) who rode in Wild West shows and taught the three Rogers children to ride and rope. Rogers Jr. and the Pittis remained friends, so it was natural in 1951 for Ben Pitti's sons, Carl and Paul, and their wives to move to Rogers's property to care for the horses and stables. Later, Ben and Ethel Pitti purchased Will Rogers Jr.'s property with their stunt-man son Carl and his wife, Mickey. They chose a hillside acre to build Carl's family home, with Ben and Ethel remaining in the house below. Local master craftsman Stan Stronks built the new home on Wrightcrest. They then sold nine acres to Venice Boulevard developers Stone & Stone, who acquired additional property as well.

Culver Crest was a 1950s annexation to Culver City. Developer Lou Crank acquired the land and developed the area, which has come to be known as the "upper crest." The property was located in the county of Los Angeles, which only had cesspools, so Crank worked to get it annexed to Culver City, which already had sewers. The intent was to develop high-end housing on a hill, with nice views. The area known as the lower crest (farther down the hill) and El Marino/Blanco Park were developed by R.J. Blanco. At the very top of the hill sits the Youngworth mansion. The mansion was given landmark status by the city through its historic preservation ordinance, which was adopted in 1991. Today, the Youngworth mansion is part of Marycrest Manor, a retirement home owned by the Catholic Archdiocese of Los Angeles. According to the Historic Preservation Advisory Committee (HPAC) document and a short history of the property available from the property owners, Leo Youngworth was an attorney in Los Angeles. He cut a trail to the top of the hill and leveled the site to build his home about 1930. Little is known of Youngworth, except that bankruptcy forced him to sell the property in 1934.

In earlier days, the property was a part of Rancho La Ballona, later in the county of Los Angeles when ground was first broken. It became a part of the Marycrest annexation to Culver City in 1965.

Carl Pitti shared becoming acquainted with Mr. Youngworth when he and friend Martin Matheson rode horses in the area. Martin, a student and football player at USC at the time, liked a particular horse, which Youngworth gave to Martin. Carl recalled Dead Horse Canyon as being just east of the Youngworth property. Youngworth, whom Pitti described simply as a nice man, was a commercial avocado grower as well. According to Carl, Martin worked for Youngworth during his student days, weeding around the trees in the avocado orchards to facilitate irrigation. Although Youngworth fed the wild turkeys, which nested at the edge of the avocado groves, the turkeys never became a commercial venture. However, Pitti speculated that they probably made it onto many local Thanksgiving tables.

The hilltop Spanish Colonial Youngworth mansion was built by Los Angeles attorney Leo Youngworth about 1930. Culver City designated the structure with landmark status in 1991.

After Youngworth left, the property took on a colorful history. While it continued to produce avocados, it also became the home of a foreign ambassador, during which time it was supposedly a front for gambling and bootlegging operations. There are claims that it was occupied by royalty, as well as noted opera singer Grace Moore. During World War II, it housed U.S. Army forces.

The last owner of the property was Lou Crank, who purchased it in 1945 and lived there with his wife, Esther, until 1954. Esther's brother was Tony Carnero, who owned the gambling ship *Rex* off the Santa Monica coast. Crank was the developer of Culver Crest in the 1950s. He named the streets, including Youngworth Street, Esterina Way (for his wife) and, of course, Cranks Road. Lou and Esther Crank divorced and sold the property, and Mr. Crank moved to another home on Culver Crest. He remarried and eventually moved to Tonga.

The Youngworth mansion opened in 1956 as Marycrest Manor Retirement and Convalescent Home. Since that time, the retirement home has constructed additional space to increase its capacity. The mansion itself was designed in the Spanish Colonial style and dates back to about 1930. Its HPAC landmark status is attributed to its architecture, age and associations.

In researching the history of Holy Cross Cemetery, the first step was checking Culver City's records. The initial entry in the building department's file appears in 1964, the year Fox Hills was annexed to Culver City. At that time, only a portion of Holy Cross was located within city limits. The majority of the cemetery was located in a portion of Los Angeles County that was later annexed to Culver City.

A May 26, 1939 issue of *The Tidings* Catholic newspaper ran an article that told of the upcoming Memorial Day opening of a new cemetery on the west side of Los Angeles. It was dedicated on Tuesday, May 30, 1939, at 3:30 p.m. The article gave a description of the new Holy Cross Cemetery as 180 acres "laid out in lawns, roads and landscaping."

The next reference of note came in the form of a March 20, 1961 internal document of the Los Angeles Archdiocese titled "Notes for Announcement of Dedication of Holy Cross Mausoleum." The document listed the date of the mausoleum dedication as Saturday, April 8, 1961, at 10:00 a.m. His eminence Cardinal McIntyre blessed the chapel and presided over a solemn Mass. Other participants in the dedication festivities included Most Reverend Timothy Manning, who gave the sermon; Right Reverend Monsignor Benjamin Hawkes, secretary to the cardinal, who acted as master of ceremonies; and Right Reverend Monsignor Edward Wade, director of cemeteries, who served as celebrant of the solemn Mass.

Montgomery and Mullay were the architects of the mausoleum, and the J.A. McNeil Company was the contractor. According to the records, the style was a "blending of modern with the traditional, an imposing façade lifting heavenward." The large sculptured fiberglass crucifixion group on the façade was created by artist Steven Zakian and executed by Emil Lorenzoni. The mausoleum building was constructed entirely of reinforced concrete. The chapel, which is located in the center and serves as the focal point, was dedicated as the "Sanctuary of the Risen Christ" with the galleria of the Angels, a second-floor corridor encircling the sanctuary. The mausoleum is adorned with a harmonious blend of imported marbles, including travertine, topaz, Rose Tavernelle, Carrara, French Rouge Antique, Saint Floriant Rose and Botticino. The individual halls were named after religious events such as the Last Supper, the Annunciation, the Resurrection, etc. The same subjects are portrayed in the stained-glass windows that face each hall and private family room. The windows were prepared at the Paris studios of Max Ingrand under the direction of Richard Jung and Paul Phillips of Pasadena. The 1961 mausoleum provided for the entombment of 6,500.

Fox Hills Mall during its construction in 1974. The area was part of the 1964 Fox Hills Annexation. The mall, now a Westfield property, was part of the first major redevelopment project in Culver City. Beyond are Holy Cross and Hillside Memorial Park, two cemeteries in Fox Hills that were also annexed from the county.

Although there is activity listed on Culver City records after 1961, the permits are sparse. In 1966, the owner was listed as the Roman Catholic archbishop, and the permit was issued for road and site grading. Later work was done in 1972, and in 1982, permits were given for the construction of a wall, gate, roadway and landscaping. The next large construction was in the county and consisted of a new chapel of the Holy Redeemer and Garden Mausoleum. Cardinal Roger Mahony officiated over the February 27, 1994 dedication. Art treasures in the form of life-size Carrara marble statues of St. Anthony and the Blessed Mother can be found in the new facility, and the Stations of the Cross are made of quarry tile, textured aluminum and sandblasted cedar. The new structure added 4,800 crypt spaces.

Holy Cross Cemetery was constructed on part of Rancho La Ballona, which was founded by Agustín Machado in partnership with his brother Ygnacio and Felipe and Tomas Talamantes. Many of the early settlers buried their families at cemeteries like Woodlawn in Santa Monica before

Holy Cross opened in 1939 to serve the Catholic community. Bing Crosby and Mario Lanza are just two of the famous names in Holy Cross.

Hillside Memorial Park was dedicated as a Jewish cemetery in 1941 after ten Jewish leaders financed the original purchase of land. The first major improvements came ten years after its founding, as a small garden mausoleum, the Garden of Memories, was constructed. The next construction was in the form of the south wing of the mausoleum and the Al Jolson Memorial. Renowned architects Paul Williams and Robert Kleigman designed those first structures. The Jolson Memorial is perhaps the most recognizable structure on the grounds. Al Jolson (1886–1950), a celebrated singer/entertainer for forty years, enjoyed a popular career spanning from stage to early phonograph recordings. He made film history in 1927 acting the title role in the Oscar winner *The Jazz Singer*, the first film with sound. His popularity continued through the '30s and '40s. Other garden areas, mausoleums and lawn crypts were added as Hillside became well known for its service to the Jewish community. By the mid-1950s, it was acquired by Temple Israel of Hollywood. The synagogue continues to operate Hillside today.

According to Hillside Memorial Park literature, it has the reputation on the Westside as the preferred resting place for the Jewish community, including many entertainment personalities. In addition to Jolson, other famous permanent residents include:

Jack Benny (1894–1974), who was one of America's great comedians. Benny, a master of timing and forever "39," was the famous violin-playing miser who played opposite his comedienne wife, Mary Livingstone (1906–1983).

Ben Blue (1901–1975), a vaudeville comedian who also appeared in short films for Warner Brothers and Hal Roach in the '20s and '30s.

Eddie Cantor (1892–1964), another memorable vaudeville comic who charmed fans with his large eyes and talent moving from stage to film, radio and television. Cantor worked on MGM's Culver City backlot to film *Forty Little Mothers*.

Jeff Chandler (1918–1961), a screen actor whose real name was Ira Grossel.

Mark Goodson (1915–1992), of the successful production team of Goodson and Todman, famed for TV shows such as *I've Got a Secret*, *The Price Is Right* and *What's My Line*.

This local landmark is located within Hillside Memorial Park in what became the Fox Hills area of Culver City. The memorial to actor/singer Al Jolson was designed by noted architect Paul Williams. *Courtesy of Hillside Memorial Park.*

Allan Sherman (1924–1973), the voice of Dr. Seuss's animated "Cat in the Hat" and a comic well known for his satirical songs in the '60s, including the Grammy-winning "Hello Mudduh, Hello Fadduh."

Other personalities include David Janssen, George Jessel, Selma Diamond, Max Factor, Lorne Greene, Dinah Shore, Mickey Cohen, Percy Faith, Arthur Freed, Moe Howard, Vic Morrow, Jerry Rubin, Sam Lerner and Hal March.

POST OFFICES

The first post office in this area was the Machado Post Office, which was located inside the Saenz family dry goods store in 1876. It was situated at the northwest corner of what is now Overland Avenue and Washington Boulevard. Many "homegrowns" remember Ships restaurant at that corner (now Starbucks, etc.).

In later times, there were post offices on Main Street and in the Washington Building, which sits between Washington and Culver Boulevards. The Gateway Station was built in 1940 during the tenure of postmaster Paul Jarrett. There are several ideas regarding the naming of the facility, but the most plausible is the one offered by Steve Newton. Steve's father, who worked for the U.S. Postal Service, said Jarrett told the employees in 1946 that it was the "Gateway to the Stars." Jarrett, who was decorated for his war service with a Purple Heart and by France with the Legion of Honor medal, served as city clerk in Culver City from 1928 to 1939 and postmaster for the following twenty years.

According to the Culver City Historic Preservation Advisory Committee report compiled by Thirtieth Street Architects and adopted by the city council in 1991, the Gateway Station, located at 9942 Culver Boulevard, is described as Moderne in style and is

> *1½ stories high, with a symmetrical façade and a flat roof, bordered with a rounded ledge. The center of interest is the wide, recessed entry porch on the north side. Four rounded columns with banded caps support the ceiling. Metal-framed, multi-paned glass panels, which run from floor to ceiling, cover the entire surface of the back wall of the porch. A pair of metal-framed doors in the center lead to the lobby. A pair of very large and unusual metal and opaque glass lanterns are placed on the concrete piers on each side of the steps. Matching round columns in recessed sections add interest to both the east and west sides of the building.*

Although the city's historic preservation ordinance, which follows the U.S. secretary of the interior's guidelines, has offered little protection of this structure, there is still some interesting history within the building. There was a congressional office off the lobby for U.S. representative Julian Dixon.

Mr. Samerjan was born in Boston in 1915. He is listed as a faculty member of Occidental College in Los Angeles in 1940. Samerjan served as a documentary artist for the U.S. Air Force in the Arctic and other locations

The Gateway Station Post Office on Culver Boulevard, just a block west of Culver City Hall, opened in 1940. The historic structure was designated with "significant" status by the Culver City Council in 1991.

and worked for the *Los Angeles Times* as an art director. He also taught art at New York University for twenty-five years. Samerjan is credited with the design of three U.S. postage stamps commemorating the Arctic, the Erie Canal and Adlai Stevenson. His other post office murals include one in Maywood, which was destroyed, and one in Calexico. The mural in the Gateway Station is titled *Studio Lot.* It is a twelve- by ten-foot mural relating empty movie sets on an MGM backlot.

There is a structure located a block west of the Gateway Station (corner of Lincoln and Culver) that was used as an annex to the Gateway Station at one time. The Jefferson Post Office at Machado Road is the newest postal facility in Culver City and serves as the main post office.

CHAPTER 3

THE BUSINESS OF BUILDING AND DEVELOPMENT

CULVER HOTEL

The Culver Hotel opened in 1924, as headlines in *Culver City Daily News*'s September 4 issue read: "City Packed with Visitors for Opening of Culver Skyscraper." The six-story hotel, then known as Hotel Hunt, was called the "latest monument to his [Harry Culver's] vision." Culver's second-floor office is now restored and used for meetings. Culver hired the Los Angeles firm of Curlett & Beelman to design the hotel. The firm specialized in large commercial structures like the Park Plaza Hotel, the Hollywood Roosevelt Hotel and the Union Oil buildings on West Seventh Street in downtown Los Angeles. Beelman went on to design the Eastern Columbia Building and the Thalberg Administration Building at MGM (1938).

The wedge-shaped Renaissance Revival–style Culver Hotel is constructed from concrete and brick with mahogany and walnut interiors. It was built on property in the center of downtown on what has been called "the shortest Main Street in the USA." Culver City's first movie theater was located on this site, and its second floor served as the first city offices. The city moved its offices nearby to Van Buren Place, and a new movie theater, the Meralta, was built on the site of today's Meralta Plaza to make way for this new landmark hotel. It was the tallest structure between the "pueblo" of Los Angeles and Abbot Kinney's resort of Venice.

Over the years, the hotel has become recognizable from the many movies filmed here, including Laurel and Hardy shorts like *Putting Pants on Philip*

With Venice Boulevard in front, look down Main Street to identify Culver's six-story Hotel Hunt (later Culver Hotel) on the right. The Adams Hotel appears opposite, and beyond on the left is Thomas Ince's second studio in the city. Beyond the bowling alley (right), Culver Grammar School is visible, with the Washington (now West End) Hotel beyond.

(1927). Numerous stars such as Red Skelton, Clark Gable, Joan Crawford, Greta Garbo and Ronald Reagan maintained part-time residences here. In a 1989 interview at a Culver City Historical Society event at The Culver Studios, actor Jerry Maren recalled this hotel as the home of the "Munchkins" when *The Wizard of Oz* was filmed in the late 1930s. Maren, who played the "Lollipop Kid," quipped that their size allowed three to fit in a bed. He remembered arriving around midnight and was excited to awaken to a band playing in the morning. He and the rest of the Munchkins who were gathered together for the first time thought they were being honored until they looked out their windows to see the Armistice Day Parade marching by.

The hotel was once owned by John Wayne, who donated it to the Los Angeles YMCA. Red Skelton and Fred McMurray have also been listed as owners. The hotel declined over the years, but Lou Catlett, general partner of Historic Hollywood Properties, rescued it from real estate speculators who had allowed it to deteriorate. The amazing restoration, which included the reconfiguration to allow for bathrooms in each room (not at the end of the hall as originally built) and seismic retrofitting, was accomplished in partnership with the Culver City Redevelopment Agency in the 1990s. However, it was not until the current owners took over and engaged local Douglas Newton to complete the restoration that the Culver Hotel returned to its former glory. The hotel is protected with landmark status under the city's historic preservation ordinance and is listed on the National Register of Historic Places. It also belongs to the Historic Hotels of America program.

A visit to the Culver Hotel only reinforces the importance of historic preservation and its economic benefits to the owner and the city. And manager Seth Horowitz enjoys talking about four stars, too!

ADAMS HOTEL

Cities develop. Buildings age. Urban blight becomes a reality. Whole blocks face demolition and the empty space becomes a parking lot. Before redevelopment occurs, people often forget what was there before. Such is the case with the block across from The Culver Studios and Culver Hotel. Over the years, that block has boasted a printer, a hotel, restaurants, bars, a liquor store—and the list goes on.

Many remember the Adams Hotel at the western edge of that block, which was situated across Main Street from the entrance to the Culver Hotel. In a 1937 directory, it was listed at 3896 Main Street, with a manager by the name of Val Reinmuth. After checking out the name, it appears that Val and his wife, Kate, were listed as living there. In the 1942 telephone directory, the hotel had an Ardmore telephone number and an ad that boasted, "Newly decorated—furnished and carpeted." By 1949, the manager was Arth Sleeper (really!), and ten years later, the Ardmore number had been replaced by a Vermont telephone number, and Finn Bjerknes was in charge.

The door to Big Ed's was on the corner of Washington and Main, on the first floor of the Adams Hotel. It was known for its long wooden bar. Normally, locals offer a lot of help with recollections, but there has always been some resistance on this one. With a twinkle in his eye, a local named Fred recalls, "My wife wouldn't let me go there" but goes on to say it has not been easy to "research." From bits and pieces, it appears that the ground-floor attraction began as Frank's Restaurant, which was run by Theresa Calcagnini.

The city's committee on permits and licenses approved an application in 1964 for Sarna's Lounge, which also offered a pool table and bowling machine for amusement. The lounge went out of business in 1980, but Sarna's Inc. transitioned the corner space into Big Ed's. Stories about that bar do exist, but mostly in hushed whispers. Some claim there was gambling in the back with a quick exit out to "Hogan's Alley," which paralleled Washington Boulevard. Local gentlemen took delight in addressing the waitresses as "doll," which got the usual response of, "Don't you 'doll' me!" The jukebox blared country music, draft beer was sold by the pitcher and trophy antlers/horns hung over the long bar. (Unidentified sources were clearly neither hunters nor cowboys!) Lynn, who lived nearby, needed to investigate it "for historic reasons" before it closed and reported that she found the regulars to be "good, congenial biker types" who enjoyed a little pool. She added that her neighbor Lee, a former math teacher, had all the angles and surprised the guys with her command of a pool cue.

The now-empty block was slated for redevelopment in 1999, but time will tell what will happen since California pulled the plug on redevelopment agencies in 2012.

CITIZEN BUILDING

After Eugene and Kitty Donovan purchased the land at 9355 Culver Boulevard, they chose the architectural firm of Orville E. Clark to design the Citizen Building—with Mrs. Donovan's input. The Donovans, natives of San Francisco, survived the great earthquake and fire of 1906 and built the Citizen Building to San Francisco's earthquake building codes, as Southern California had yet to adopt guidelines. In 1928, the firm of O'Hanlon and Flansburg began construction on the Citizen Building. Eugene Donovan's final instructions before work began were reportedly, "Wherever possible, all materials, supplies and labor will be obtained from local sources in Culver City."

Construction was completed in 1929 at a cost of $80,000 (which included furnishings), and the News Printing Company that had been established in 1923 under the management of Eugene Donovan's son Roy and the *Western Citizen*, founded by Eugene Donovan, were consolidated into Citizen Publishers and Printers. Before completion of the new building, the Donovans' business had been located across the street, initially on Bagley, around the corner. The "new" twenty-page edition of the *Citizen* was printed on December 6, 1929, in its brand-new, modern plant. The newspaper was "dedicated in perpetuity to the service of the people that no good cause shall lack a champion and that evil shall not thrive unopposed." On January 1, 1930, the Donovans hosted a public opening for more than two thousand guests in the *Citizen*'s new home. The Donovans' dream of a completely self-contained, successful hometown newspaper and commercial printing plant had become a reality in just seven short years. Their accounts included Thomas Ince, Hal Roach, MGM, Selznick, RKO, Pathe and DeMille Studios.

The award-winning *Citizen* was a dynamic force in the development of the community, spurring better government and business, recreational facilities, adequate streets, lighting and other projects that factor into an ideal modern community. Donovan championed battles for adequate bus transportation, the modernization and improvement of the fire and police departments and beneficial zoning regulations. He was also an advocate for the chamber of commerce. In 1934, before the Hollywood and Culver City Chambers of Commerce "buried the hatchet," Donovan ran a contest to rename Culver City, since movie credits at that time did not read "Made in Culver City." Entries for the ten-dollar prize included names like "Cinema City" and "Filmville." Needless to say, the city retained its Culver City name.

This rendering depicts the Citizen Building, which housed the publishers of the *Citizen* newspaper in downtown Culver City. Built in 1929 by the Donovan family, it was the first structure in Culver City to be placed on the National Register of Historic Places. *Courtesy of the Donovan family.*

Eugene Donovan learned printing and publishing in his native San Francisco. He was the managing editor of the *Reno Gazette* and was affiliated at various times with the *Call*, the *Examiner* and other San Francisco dailies before he moved to Southern California. Before he established his own newspaper in Culver City, Donovan was the publisher and managing editor of the *Culver City Daily News*.

Eugene and Catherine Donovan both died in 1948 and were survived by their son and grandson. The *Citizen* remained a family-owned business, with grandson Roy L. Donovan still active in the community until its sale in the late 1990s. Bound copies of the *Citizen* can be found at Loyola-Marymount University.

Josetta Sbeglia purchased and renovated the Citizen Building in the 1990s. As of 2012, the Citizen Building has new owners who also have respect for historic structures.

The Citizen Building was marked by the Culver City Historical Society as Historic Site No. 4 in 1984. In 1987, it became the first structure in Culver City to be placed on the National Register of Historic Places. It also carries local landmark status by action of the Culver City Council. The building is known for its fusion of Beaux Arts classical elements and Art Deco. Other examples of this type of architecture in the downtown area, like the 1928 City Hall and Fire Station No. 1, were demolished.

HULL BUILDING

After Culver City incorporated in 1917, the city trustees went about the business of legislating for city operation. One such action in 1919, Resolution #57, appointed Dr. Foster Hull as the second city health officer, replacing Dr. Mortensen. The Hull Building was built by the same Dr. Hull in 1925 as the first hospital in Culver City. It became a victim of the Depression in the 1930s but was acquired by Louis Freeman, whose family still retains ownership.

Although its uses have changed numerous times over the years, the Hull Building retains most of its original character. Its many occupants have included Freeman Furniture, Sunset Drug, Ed Tinger's Culver City Flowers, Al Simon's Sada's Flowers, Kamin's Shoes, a boardinghouse on the second floor, the Bank of Orange County, Riccardo's Restaurant, Bella Pasta, San Gennaro and, most recently, Akasha. Office space over the years housed Dauber Security and offices for production companies, including Sony Pictures. By council action, the Hull Building was awarded landmark status in 1991 with adoption of the first city historic preservation ordinance. The outside of the structure is protected, although it probably would not be a candidate for the National Register

An early look at Culver City's downtown area, where the "Culver-Washington X" existed. The picture shows off the landmark Hull Building (left) with the historic Culver Hotel straight ahead. The shorter structure just beyond is the Adams Hotel. *Courtesy of the Freeman family.*

of Historic Places due to the alterations of the windows. The architecture is recognized as Neo-Classical in style, with construction materials of tan and rose-colored brick.

The Bank of Orange County, a tenant in 1978, gutted the Hull Building to bring it up to earthquake standards. This explains its minimal damage from the 1994 Northridge earthquake. Some bricks dislodged and fell during the temblor, and coincidentally, there was a brick building in the block west of The Culver Studios, which had similar brick. That structure was being demolished for the construction of the new Culver Studios office building, and careful examination by owner Sony Pictures determined that the bricks were not only similar but made by the same manufacturer as those in the Hull Building. Sony Pictures saved enough brick for the Freeman family to make the needed repairs.

The Hull Building was recognized by the Culver City Historical Society as Historic Site No. 2, as evidenced by the plaque on the building. Louis Freeman's son, Bert Freeman, was in attendance at the marking. Louis's grandson Stu Freeman, of Freeman Property Management, still maintains a presence in town and is an active member and past president of the Culver City Historical Society.

WASHINGTON BUILDING

The Washington Building was commissioned by Charles E. Lindblade. Its two-year construction began in 1926. Lindblade, for whom a Culver City street was named, was a business associate of the city's founder, Harry H. Culver. The master builders were Orlopp and Orlopp, who were listed on site in 1927. The building designer was Arthur D. Scholz, with Orville L. Clark mentioned in old records as the probable consulting architect. Clark went on to design other local buildings including city hall in 1928 and the fire station next door. The Washington Building was described by Carson Anderson in the owner's application for the National Register of Historic Places as "Builder's Beaux Arts Classicism." The foundation and walls are both reinforced concrete. Anderson felt the areas of significance of the building fell into the categories of architecture, commerce and community planning and development. The period of significance on the form was considered to be 1926–1940, with Lindblade listed as the significant person.

Lindblade (1887–1940), a real estate developer, served both as vice-president and president of Harry Culver's real estate firm. The Washington Building was constructed during Lindblade's most notable years professionally when he and Culver actively developed Culver City. These also appear to be his most visible years in the community. Some of his activities listed in the 1929 *Who's Who in California* included service as a director of Security First National Bank of Los Angeles and Pacific Building and Loan Association, which financed much of the city's early development. He also served on the board of the Pacific Military Academy and was a founding member of the Culver City Chamber of Commerce. He served as president of the Culver City Realty Board in 1927 and director of the California Real Estate Association in 1928–29. He and his wife, Joan Fox Lindblade, lived in nearby Cheviot Hills.

The two-story Washington Building reportedly cost $30,000 at construction. Its triangular shape earned it the nickname the "Flatiron Building," although it was twenty stories short of the famous twenty-two-story Flatiron Building in New York. The structure occupies 135 feet of Washington Boulevard frontage and stretches 152 feet along Culver Boulevard. The two long sides converge to a flattened east wall of 12 feet (where Starbucks is located), while the west wall measures 68 feet wide.

The building housed the local post office until the Gateway Station was completed down the street in 1940. Other notable occupants of the building included the World War II Draft Board; the MGM Fan Club (after the war); a dentist, Dr. Connelly; the American National Insurance Co.; attorney F.A.

Looking west from the Culver Hotel with Culver Boulevard on the left and Washington on the right of the historic Washington Building. The Hull Building appears lower right, and just beyond the triangular Washington Building (right) is the Culver Theatre. In the distance, MGM Studios, the first of the three major studios built in Culver City, can be seen with its historic sign atop the first soundstages at that studio. The water tower is also a part of the studioscape.

Berry; photographer Chester Graves; and the Lindblade Real Estate and Development Company (1929–1932.) The Washington Building is protected by its landmark status and is also listed on the National Register of Historic Places. BYCO, a longtime family-owned Culver City business, applied for the National Register status.

LEGION BUILDING

The building located on Hughes known as the Legion Building was constructed by the American Legion Post #46 as its clubhouse in 1930. Culver City building department records show the contractor as Don S. Ely, famed builder of St. Augustine's Church. It was listed as a "2-story class-D Club House" on the permit.

The landmark Legion Building was constructed over the first swimming pool in Culver City. Although the American Legion is located in another structure today, the legion hall was the center of the social scene in the early days. It was constructed on land donated by city founder Harry Culver.

The Culver City Historical Society placed a bronze marker on the structure in 1985, making it Historic Site No. 5. Subsequently, Culver City designated the building as a "significant" historic structure. Its survey refers to the Legion Building at 3824 Hughes as Spanish Colonial style. A 1937 local telephone directory listed the American Legion Community Post #46 at 3818 Hughes, with the American Legion Hall at 3820 Hughes.

According to an August 8, 1930 *Citizen* newspaper article, the Legion Building was scheduled to open to the public at noon the following day, with the dedication planned for that evening. The ceremony began at 8:00 p.m. and was followed by a dance. George Freeman's orchestra provided the music. The article also noted, "Many interesting features will mark the day, including the Legion Bugle and Drum Corps recently organized by Tom Ammerman." It added that the public "was cordially invited to inspect the beautiful new building." The legion auxiliary was in charge of refreshments.

The Legion Building was constructed over the "Culver Plunge," which was reportedly the first swimming pool in the city, and located on land donated by city founder Harry Culver. Over the years, the Legion Building became a well-known venue for entertainment. Not only did the American Legion and its auxiliary sponsor dances and events, but it was frequently used by the community. A 1956 *Citizen* article stated, "Community Post Club House on Hughes Ave. is considered one of the finest in the state, and its facilities are available at any time to members of the armed services or to any honorably discharged veteran."

The legion post eventually sold the building to the hospital next door and built a new structure on Sepulveda Boulevard. Brotman Memorial Hospital, later known as Brotman Medical Center, used the structure for storage for some time before Dr. Gerald Glantz spearheaded its renovation. The earliest permit found under the Brotman name (1975) was pulled by Chanen Construction for interior partitions. Brotman restored the inside in stages and named the second-floor auditorium the Glantz Auditorium in honor of the doctor who had saved the building.

HELMS BAKERIES

Paul Helms took an early retirement in New York for health reasons and moved his family to the temperate California climate in 1926. He began building a structure between Washington and Venice Boulevards in 1930, and Helms Bakery opened on March 2, 1931.

Helms won a contract to supply bread for the 1932 Olympics in Los Angeles. Early Helms vehicles, dubbed "coaches," sported the Olympic symbol, which is still recognizable on the historic sign atop the building. Given Paul Helms's interest in athletics, it was not surprising that he, Bill Schroeder and Syd Kronenthal established the Helms Athletic Foundation, an incredible athletic museum/library. Culver High's football field still carries the name of Helms Field.

Helms Bakery grew over the years, as the familiar whistle of the Helms coaches delighted locals as the vehicles traversed the southland as far north as Fresno, east to San Bernardino, south to San Diego and up to the moon! In

Helms "coaches," which operated at Helms Bakeries in Culver City from 1931 to 1969, brought smiles to locals who heard the famed whistle entering their neighborhoods. This shot looks from Venice to Washington Boulevard with the Baldwin Hills in the distance.

1969, an aggressive marketing campaign netted Helms a contract to furnish the first bread on the moon via Apollo 11. The Helms motto, "Daily to Your Door," is still inscribed on the building. Although their products were never sold in stores, Helms Bakeries became a major employer in the city.

Paul Helms earned the admiration and respect of his employees—his "co-worker family." In a 1997 interview, Paul Helms III proclaimed, "The key to the bakery's success was the co-worker concept." As Helms walked through the plant, he called each of his co-workers by his or her first name. In August 1969, twelve years after Paul Helms's death, the bakery closed. Lifestyle patterns had changed. More women were entering the workforce, and insurance issues, union pressures and the competition of supermarkets forced the family to close the bakery.

For more than thirty years, Helms employees continued to meet at an annual summer picnic. Some years, the picnic was held in the building, with the welcoming Helms logo at the entry and a vintage coach's drawers overflowing with donuts. Attendees included former Helms employees, Mr. and Mrs. Paul Helms III, city council members, building owner Walter Marks III, Olympic champion Olga Connolly and Syd Kronenthal.

Helms's Zigzag Moderne–style building still stands proudly in two cities—partly in Culver City and partly in Los Angeles. The imposing bronze Helmsman that stood in the center of Venice Boulevard was moved to Chace Park in nearby Marina del Rey. The building, recognized by Culver City as a landmark structure, was marked as Historic Site No. 9 by the Culver City Historical Society in 1997, as evidenced by the bronze plaque on Helms Avenue.

Today, the Helms Building is part of a thriving commercial center owned by Walter N. Marks, Inc., another family venture. The occupants advertise it as part of the Helms Furniture District, which once included the Antique Guild, the Jazz Bakery, Gascon Theatre, La Dijonaise and more. In current times, H.D. Buttercup anchors the north side, and the Marks family eventually extended the renovations to the Beacon Laundry building.

SHOPPING

Harry Culver established the center of Culver City with his 1913 filing of Main Street with Los Angeles County. This also determined the first shopping district. Progress was evident just a decade later. The little Main Street was meant for walking—and a little driving. But attention was paid to making it open, complete with a grassy center median, trees and even a flagpole. Does that sound familiar? In early times, one could find hardware stores, plumbing shops, a bakery, department stores, shoe stores, grocery stores, banks and more.

The longest-standing retailer on Main Street was established in 1923 as Steller Bros. & Skoog by the original owners, Adolph W. Steller, Herman A. Steller and John L. Skoog. Active chamber member Adolph Steller was, in fact, presiding over the chamber of commerce during the development of the Hayden Tract, the first industrial tract in Culver City. Steller proactively marketed the tract in the mid-1940s, which explains the street carrying his name.

The original addresses on Main Street were numbered in the 7000s, with the early Steller Bros. & Skoog listed at 7024. As Culver City developed, the town was laid out south of Venice Boulevard, but in many locations, the boundaries are mid-block. Main Street is one of those streets, and the early store was just "across the alley," north of its current location. That store was actually in Los Angeles's jurisdiction, which begins at Bagley Avenue.

After World War II, Caryll Wild, the store bookkeeper since 1938, purchased the store with Jim Bohn, and the name was simplified to Stellar Hardware.

Caryll Wild and his wife, Marguerite, continued the tradition of active participation in the community. In 1968, a young navy pilot named Rob Barber married their daughter Jan, and in 1972, Jan's sister Charlyn married youthful high school shop teacher Jack Barton. In 1973, brothers-in-law Rob and Jack bought the hardware store and continued to foster the casual hometown hardware store atmosphere. In keeping with our Screenland history, Rob and Jack fought their first impulse to paint Marilyn Monroe on the back of the store. Greatly loved Laurel and Hardy won out, with Stan and Ollie in overalls, of course!

When prompted, Jack spoke of their most unusual sale, a request from Larry Flynt Publications. Flynt needed eight five-gallon barrels immediately. The store had no empties, so Jack and Rob put a sign in the window offering free paint thinner and kerosene to those who brought their own containers. The store emptied containers for happy customers, and Larry Flynt got his barrels for a pontoon-type boat to float a lady in a photo shoot.

Rob and Jack both cite their most memorable day in business as January 17, 1994, when they came to work after the Northridge earthquake. They found the windows broken out and two-thirds of their stock on the floor. That day, many of their old-time customers showed up in overalls to help. Others were so thankful the store was open that they arrived with turkey and ham to feed the employees. Rob called it "the most gratifying day ever."

Although "Lion Jack" and "Rotarian Rob" remain a presence in Culver City, their 2008 liquidation sale retired the "smiling boys in short pants" and the ever-welcoming smell of popcorn.

Downtown Culver City

Henry Culver built his Hotel Hunt (now Culver Hotel) and moved his offices there upon completion. The six-story "skyscraper" dwarfed the Adams Hotel across the street. Beyond, Thomas Ince had built his second studio in Culver City, which remains today. Proudly reminiscent of Mount Vernon, the "mansion" housed his second-floor offices. This was downtown Culver City in the 1920s.

The Culver Center, which offered a new, larger shopping venue, became a reality after World War II. The Culver City Redevelopment Agency (CCRA) was established in 1971, and in the fall of 1975, the first major CCRA project opened its doors—the Fox Hills Mall. It has since gone through redevelopment as the Westfield Shopping Town, Fox Hills.

In 1991, the CCRA turned an eye back to Main Street and sponsored a charette—a new word to locals. The intent of that exercise was to look at the city's original "downtown" and decide on a plan. The charette took place on a March weekend. It began on a Friday night with an orientation session at the Veterans Memorial Auditorium, complete with a slide show featuring examples of other downtowns. On Saturday, 125 residents and businesspeople took an "awareness walk" through the deteriorating downtown area with staff and shared their thoughts back at the auditorium in the afternoon. The Technical Resource Team presented its recommendations on Sunday to the agency, charette participants and staff. The process was led by James Cloar, principal of LDR International. The end result pointed to strengths such as "lots of space," "entertainment industry," "location," "landmark buildings," "citizens' pride and spirit" and "the width of Culver Boulevard." The weaknesses came in the form of comments like "a lack of visual appeal," "pedestrian un-friendly," "need for convenient parking," "no sense of center," "traffic patterns" and "building conditions."

The workshop participants thought the roles of downtown Culver City should be those of "civic focal point," "social gathering place," "business center" and "image-setter." To achieve these roles, specific uses were listed as "better retail, professional offices, residential, cultural and entertainment, restaurants, town square, civic uses, greenery and open space, family attractions, and transition to nearby neighborhoods." Some specific uses often mentioned were a farmers' market, hotel, roller rink and a child care facility. Themes agreed upon for future planning included "film land, crossroads of the stars, small town, diversity of lifestyles and functions, landscaping and user-friendly." It's taken some time, but take a walk today and see how input from local citizens guided a process that is still on track!

CULVER CENTER

The second major shopping area in Culver City was a post–World War II development called the Culver Center. Completed in 1950, it was one of the first shopping centers in Southern California. It quickly became feared competition for the original Main Street businesses. In fact, the city council refused May Company's request to build one of its department stores there. Present-day Ralph's was originally the site of a Market Basket. Women's clothing stores included the Oliver family's first Ames, a Quist's, Her Nibs, Charlestons, Trend O'Fashion, Charlene's, Cindy's, Mode O'Day and Anita's. Eskridge's Culver Center Flowers was located in the center, as were the New York Bakery, Bert's Men's Store, Lerner's, Crosby's, Hellman Hardware, Holland's Draperies, Singer Sewing Machine Center (later the House of Fabrics and Joann's), the Sportsmen's Exchange, Western Auto, Center Deli and, later, Lindy's Deli. Shoe stores were plentiful and included Karl's, Berland's, Comar's, Stride-Rite and Paige Family Shoes. There was Culver Center Beauty Salon, Shoe Repair, Cleaners, Stationers and Department Store. J.C. Penney and a W.T. Grants—a dime store with a soda fountain— were on the same side as today's Sit and Sleep. Other establishments included a drugstore, one of three run by the Wellington brothers, and a Thrifty Drugs (now Rite Aid). Martin's Music was a popular family-owned record store. Curry's, with its huge ice cream cone outside, was also a busy place. There were Torrey's and Gray's Jewelers, a Bank of America and Security Bank. The Culver Center merchants formed a strong association in early days and successfully fought a proposed Naradel development for a discount store (Zody's) and forty retail stores at Washington and Overland.

In earlier days, Culver Center Street was called Hacienda Street. At the eastern edge of Culver Center (now Starbucks) was a Ships restaurant, but in 1874, it was the Machado Post Office, located inside the Saenz family dry goods store. In 1992 and 1996 interviews with Ray Moselle, retired CCFD battalion chief, he related arriving by freight train for the 1932 Olympics. His brother was a professional fighter who lived in the Boxing Arena, so Ray moved in with him. In 1935, Ray found himself sweeping the arena for rent money. The arena was located on the Culver Center site, and fighters like Fred Fulton, Jack Dempsey and middleweight Nish Kerkorian competed there. Kerkorian's brother Kirk, who later bought MGM, was an amateur welterweight. Their parents owned a bar on Washington Boulevard near Adams. Fred Machado's uncle, Johnny McManus, also fought there. On Monday nights, Mae West had a front-row seat next to Pearl Merrill, one of the owners of the Meralta Theater (and Saenz's sister), and Lorene Furrow, a young teacher who later married councilman Leroy Koos. With the movie studios nearby, many stars were regulars, including Lupe Velez, who often yelled from her ringside seat, "You need to chop wood!" if a fighter was out of shape. The Culver City Stadium burned down, but it too had its place in history, as Sy Saenz provided an athletic venue and helped a lot of boys get back on track.

Culver Center was a post–World War II development that opened in 1950. This photo shows the southeast edge of Culver Center, where Ships restaurant offered affordable food and toasters at every table! Culver Center Street, which most businesses faced, was beyond the parking lot.

Moselle remembered the area from Venice south as home to Ed's Chili Parlor (owned by the Hennarty family), parking, the Culver City Stadium and a track and baseball field. Moselle pitched, and locals like Charlie Lugo played third base for the Cardinals on that semi-pro baseball field. Ed's Chili Parlor offered affordable meals. An old menu touted a "Special Spanish Dinner" for seventy-five cents that consisted of "soup, salad, chili con carne, Spanish rice, Spanish beans, enchiladas and fruit and coffee." If you just wanted a bowl of menudo, the cost was thirty-five cents.

HAYDEN TRACT

Harry Culver's dream for a balanced community included an economic base to support its residents. Main Street provided the initial retail, and the studios were the early industry. By 1922, the Honers had established the first manufacturing plant, Western Stove. It was located on Hays Street (now National Boulevard) north of La Ballona Creek along the Pacific Electric right of way. The city continued to grow until the Great Depression. In 1945, the president of the chamber of commerce was Adolph Steller, of Steller Hardware. With the end of the war, construction was possible again. Steller actively promoted an industrial area located on former Rancho Rincón de los Bueyes land. It was named the Hayden Tract. Sam Hayden, a transplanted glass manufacturer from the East Coast, was the developer. Local newspaper headlines read, "Factories Coming Here in New Development."

The Hayden Tract abutted Western Stove, which by 1947 was celebrating its silver anniversary. It had grown from two small buildings and 20 employees to a manufacturing concern with 720 employees on eleven acres. By 1949, the forty-acre Hayden Tract had become a sixty-plus-lot subdivision of "modern reinforced concrete buildings" that the *Citizen* newspaper proclaimed as "one of the finest in the world." It was designed to expand Culver City's economic base. Business owners gave easements on their properties to the railroad for spur tracks, which enhanced the manufacturers' freight car access to the Pacific Electric Railway.

Sam Hayden filed the Hayden Tract map on March 14, 1946. As with most developments, the streets were named by the developer. The Hayden Tract enhanced Culver City's economic base and offered jobs to locals. As the manufacturing plants thrived, so did they struggle. A transition occurred, as the trains no longer stopped to load and drop goods. By the early 1990s, the character of the Hayden Tract had changed. Gone were the clothing, plastic, pen and curtain manufacturers; sheet metal shops; and Mattel. Wholesalers, like Freddi's China Closet, moved in, and J.J.'s and La Dijonaise became the cafes of choice. The new wave brought the Willows Private School on Higuera, the western boundary of the tract. Many original buildings deteriorated. The Culver City Redevelopment Agency, established in 1971, turned its attention to the Hayden Tract. Property owners Frederick and Laurie Smith began to redevelop their buildings with noted architect Eric Owen Moss. The revitalization continues to draw state-of-the-art technology, media and entertainment tenants. *New Yorker* magazine featured the tract with its unusual architecture.

And so the story of Sam Hayden's tract continues, and even businesses that were not a part of the original land tract—like the Landmark Industrial Tract nearby (formerly Hal Roach Studios)—enjoy the close proximity and name association. The spirit continues today, as the Metro rail opened in 2012 on land adjacent to the Landmark Industrial Tract. Culver City began its "branding" in the 1930s, as the "Heart of Screenland" appeared on our city seal, but it has continued in the form of planned areas like the Hayden Tract and beyond.

Built by New York glass manufacturer Sam Hayden, the Hayden Tract was the first industrial tract in Culver City. This post–World War II development offered industrial space and access to railroad spurs for delivery. It was built adjacent to Western Stove, the first industrial plant in Culver City, on Hays (now National Boulevard) and extended to Higuera.

The Hayden Tract's new look shows off the work of noted architects like Eric Owen Moss.

CHAPTER 4

THE MOVIE STUDIOS

THE FIRST MAJOR STUDIO

Harry Culver combined his goal to establish a thriving community with his keen interest in the budding movie industry. The equation eventually yielded "Culver City, the Heart of Screenland."

Thomas Ince was a young but well-known filmmaker when Culver spied him making one of his westerns on Ballona Creek. It was well before "talkies," but the intrigue was there, as he watched Ince direct his painted Indians in canoes on the waterway. Culver convinced Ince to move from his Inceville studio at the beach (now Sunset and Pacific Coast Highway) to Washington Boulevard.

The first studio began with the 1915 Colonnade, the ceremonial entrance to Ince/Triangle Studios. The principals were Thomas Ince, D.W. Griffith and Mack Sennet. By 1918, however, Samuel Goldwyn took over the lot, and it became Goldwyn Studios, where Howard Dietz was creating the "Leo the Lion" logo.

The Metro-Goldwyn-Mayer merger took place in 1924, the same year Columbia Pictures was born in Hollywood. MGM rapidly grew to six working studio lots and more than 180 acres by the end of the 1930s. The studio was managed by Louis B. Mayer, a Russian immigrant. The main lot was like a city within a city, with its own police and fire departments, telegraph and post office, water tower and well, art department, laboratory

Three major movie studios are labeled in this 1937 photo, with dreams of the Veterans Memorial Building/Expo shown at right. Original plans called for a movie museum.

and backlot amenities. By the late 1920s, the glass stages gave way to soundstages (twenty-eight during MGM's tenure), with Stage #15 known as the largest in the free world and another equipped with a tank for underwater scenes. The first soundstages were completed with a proscenium arch. Mrs. Mayer, the studio chief's wife, taught the commissary chef how to make chicken and matzo ball soup to her husband's taste. A new commissary was built in the 1930s to keep productivity high on the studio lot. That structure has maintained "significant" historic status with the city since 1991. The newest commissary is now located more centrally on the studio lot.

Louis B. Mayer was close to his head of production, Irving Thalberg, the husband of actress Norma Shearer. Doug Shearer, his brother-in-law, headed the sound department. MGM released fifty films a year, and the payroll reached five thousand employees. MGM earned fame for its musicals. Mayer made provisions for his child stars (Elizabeth Taylor, Mickey Rooney, Judy Garland, etc.) to be schooled on the studio lot. Adoring locals waited for autographs at the East Gate of the studio, where Louis B. Mayer boasted the entrance of "more stars than there are in the heavens."

Looking back to the 1950s as the Red Car was heading west on the tracks in the center of Culver Boulevard. MGM Studios stands tall above the trees in the background at Madison Avenue. Photo taken on Culver and Duquesne, where Culver City Hall stood. The entrance to the police department and council chambers was noted on Duquesne. *Courtesy of Bison Archives.*

A new administration building, dedicated in 1938, was named for Irving Thalberg, who died in 1936. Thalberg, who was well known as the genius head of production, was never listed in movie credits. He was quoted as saying, "Credit you give yourself is not worth having." Louis B. Mayer grew the studio but lost power to production chief Dore Schary in 1951. MGM added TV, but the studio began a decline in the 1960s.

Kirk Kerkorian bought the studio in the 1970s. James Aubrey, the new president, stripped the studio, selling off its glorious past in an auction where the yellow brick road had once stretched for the filming of *The Wizard of Oz.* The backlots were next. Lot #2, where Mickey Rooney lived on Andy Hardy Street and Gene Kelly danced in *Singin' in the Rain*, became history. On Jefferson Boulevard, Lot #3 was sold for housing, and the "monkey farm" (where the animals were kept) and plant nursery across the street became commercial, as did the antique car lot, now Raintree Shopping Center.

MGM transitioned into MGM/UA in the 1980s, and in 1986, Turner Broadcasting bought UA and the film library and the last remaining lot became Lorimar Telepictures. MGM moved across the street to the Filmland Building, where it stayed until its 1992 move to Santa Monica.

On January 1, 1990, the studio became a part of Sony Pictures Entertainment, which made a major commitment to the Culver City community to renovate the Culver City property. The studio went through a three-year approval process while it transitioned into the forty-five-acre state-of-the-art Sony Pictures Studios and the global headquarters of Sony Pictures Entertainment (SPE). SPE entered into a long-term lease for the Filmland Building (now Sony Pictures Plaza) when MGM left. Sony Pictures reproduced the oval office for *An American President*; created movies like *Air Force One*, *Men in Black* and *Stuart Little*; and offers Sony Pictures Classics. The historic movie lot is now the home of *Jeopardy!* and *Wheel of Fortune*, and the studio continues to produce entertainment with cutting-edge technology through its Imageworks facility. Sony is also known as a wonderful corporate citizen and a supporter of the schools and cultural arts. And just as Harry Culver expected, the studio workers support local businesses from restaurants to flower shops.

Although many were saddened to lose the familiar historic sign that originally graced MGM's tall complex of Stages 3, 4, 5 and 6, Sony Pictures Entertainment, under the city's Art in Public Places Program, unveiled a new local landmark on October 1, 2012. The colorful *Rainbow* is making people smile for miles around. The artwork, created by Tony Tasset, stretches over 155 feet high in front of the landmark Thalberg Building.

STUDIO TOURS: RECOLLECTIONS OF A TOUR GUIDE

I was lucky to spend my first two summers of college (1963 and 1964) as a messenger/tour guide at MGM Studios. It was a perfect job for "a kid"—good pay and great fun. We worked out of the communications department, sorted mail and took our route twice a day. The perks included signing fan photos and taking VIP tours of the studio lots.

The tours began at the Thalberg Building, now a landmark structure. We met our guests, who could be anyone from theater chain owners to elected officials and friends of studio officials, and walked them around the main lot. At that time, Grant Avenue led in from Madison Avenue past the front of the Thalberg Building, which was named for MGM's genius head of production, to the famed East Gate. The guard at the gate's name was

Kenny Hollywood—for real! Just past the gate, the first building was then the "TV 4" Building, which housed production offices for Filmways and shows like *The Man from U.N.C.L.E.* The dentist's office was upstairs in that building. We talked about this being the first of six studio lots that totaled over 180 acres. It was like a city within a city. Along the route, we saw the commissary, which served matzo ball soup just the way studio chief Louis B. Mayer liked it. Mayer was all about productivity, and his intent was to keep the studio workers on the lot for their meals.

The script directed us to point out the doctor's offices, rehearsal halls, wardrobe and makeup, police and fire departments, the studio lab and the mill and other craft shops, as well as the early dressing rooms ("Washington Row"), which were adjacent to the Landmark Colonnade.

People enjoyed seeing the schoolhouse, where great child actors like Judy Garland, Mickey Rooney and Elizabeth Taylor studied, and many of the twenty-eight original soundstages, which yielded an opportunity to point out some of our rich history in the "Heart of Screenland." The complex of the first four soundstages had a proscenium arch for glamorous productions like the Busby-Berkeley Musicals and Ziegfeld Follies, and the nearby scoring stage was responsible for many great musicals.

The four-story property department building held everything from candlesticks to couches. During one of those summers as I was exiting that building quickly, I slipped on the steps and flew out to land on "Main Street." Earnestly carrying my mailbag in front, I knocked myself out only to "come to" with my boss standing over me in her spike heels. She had run from her office halfway across the lot. And if that wasn't embarrassing enough, Elvis Presley, who was shooting *Viva Las Vegas*, stopped to see if he could lend assistance.

After taking a small group on a tour of MGM's main lot, we had the option of hopping on the studio open-air tram to Lot #2. Wally, the tram driver, was a cheery man with wisps of strawberry blond hair escaping wildly from his cap. A quiet listener, he probably knew more about the studio than most, and he was always a help to "green" tour guides.

The guests always enjoyed seeing the outdoor sets on the backlots. As we entered Lot #2, the train station was immediately visible, and a quick right took us under the wires that held the canvas when filming a night scene during the day. "New York Eastside Street" was the first treat, but there were façades that appealed to everyone—the street where Gene Kelly danced in *Singin' in the Rain*, Mrs. Miniver's house, Esther Williams's swimming pool and Andy Hardy Street, with the church from *Father of the Bride* and *Sweet Bird of Youth*. A *National Velvet* set was across from the bridge from *Gigi*. There was a town square and

MGM's Lot #2 began at Overland Avenue (front) to Elenda Street. Culver Boulevard is off to the left beyond the railroad station façades. The three-sided building shown at the center right could be dressed as a hospital, courthouse or store, depending on the need. A New York Eastside Street began on the lower right.

a *Verona* set that was partially burned for reuse as a "bombed-out war town" in the *Combat* TV series. In the 1970s, Lot #2 was sold. It is currently home to Studio Estates, two senior housing developments and our new Senior Center on the corner of Overland and Culver.

As a youngster, I remember riding in the back seat of our family car going down Jefferson Boulevard. There was a long stretch of green fence, above which appeared a mysterious rectangle of sky—sometimes rainy, sometimes sunny. We took our studio backlots for granted. It wasn't until that college summer job that I got a look inside of MGM's Lot #3 and saw what that was all about! It was a rare opportunity to take a group down to the largest MGM backlot. It was always by limousine, and the entry was on the corner of Overland and Jefferson (now Lakeside Villas). The first visible set was a fort built for the *Gunslinger* and *Rawhide* series. Behind a Mexican village emerged the big water tower used in *How the West Was Won*. The Billy the Kid street was used for the movie of the same name, as well as *Lone Star* and *Cimarron*. In that area, one first saw replicas of the HMS *Bounty* from *Mutiny on the Bounty*.

One of the most appreciated sets was "St. Louis Street." It was easy to visualize Judy Garland walking out the door of one of the magnificent Victorian façades into the perfect front yard. The "sky" I used to admire as a kid was set over a shallow tank fitted with propellers on either side to make waves during water shots. The "jungle" was the farthest area, now known as "Raintree," and the site of Johnny Weismuller's escapades as Tarzan. For '60s TV buffs, *Combat* was filmed there, too. The famous lake was edged by a Salem Waterfront Village, used in films like *Advance to the Rear* and *All the Brothers Were Valiant*. I loved to see the showboat from the film of that name docked there next to a boat from *Tugboat Annie*.

Today, Sony Pictures offers public tours of its historic studio lot.

MORE ON THE BACKLOTS

Most local people remember Walter Cameron as the "cowboy" owner of Ben-Hur Stables. The stables were located on the southwest corner of Overland Avenue and Jefferson Boulevard from 1922 until Cameron's death in 1942. He also had property across the street, on Overland, which is where the stagecoaches and other rigs were kept. Walter Cameron is said to have made a comfortable living by supplying horses, burros and equipment for movies. He lived on the property, and his sister, Mrs. E. Briggs, took care of his house.

When Walter Cameron decided to work a little less, he sold the property across from the stables to MGM, and it became part of its largest backlot, Lot #3 (now Lakeside Villas). The stables property was eventually acquired by MGM to store its movie vehicles. It served as Lot #5 until the 1970s, but today we know it as Raintree Plaza Shopping Center.

In one 1933 newspaper article, Ben-Hur Stables was dubbed the "Stables of History." The article described the broad scope of vehicles and horse gear for rent. As for saddles, there were authentic padded ones of the hard-riding Cossacks, silver-adorned Navajo saddles, U.S. trappings of the Civil War period and one rumored to be a favorite of Rudolph Valentino. But the one that hung below a faded Mexican serape in a storeroom carried the most interesting history. It was part of the ransom paid to Pancho Villa for the release of General Luis Torres. The booty for Torres's return included this hand-tooled Mexican saddle with hammered silver ornaments. The leather had been crafted to tell stories of the Old Testament. The Smithsonian Institute has exhibited that very saddle.

What most do not realize is that Walter Cameron could be called the first movie star. Cameron played the part of the sheriff in *The Great Train Robbery*, which is credited as the first movie with a plot. His service as a U.S. marshal in Oklahoma helped him get the part. For the role of the star of the 1903 motion picture, Cameron said he received $35 in pay from the Edison Company, which produced the endeavor near Paterson, New Jersey. The movie was filmed in just five days. Cameron said that he also moved the camera, picked up props and swept the floor! He participated in the forerunner of motion picture "chases." Cameron stated in a 1938 article that the producer/director, Edwin S. Porter, also used another novelty, a "close-up" shot. The New York–based Edison Company rented the train from the Lackawanna Railroad for $45, which brought the movie's budget up to $2,000. The movie was considered quite a thriller, with a stunt shot of a dummy falling out of the train.

Walter Cameron retired from the movies in 1922 to establish his stables, which supplied his "range critters" to movies from *Ben-Hur* to *Gone with the Wind*. A veteran of more than two hundred films, Walter Cameron continued to make occasional movie appearances and later acted as an advisor.

Local resident Paul Pitti often shared that Walter Cameron was a friend of his father, performer Bennie Pitti. Paul had fond memories of going over to the Ben-Hur Stables with his dad. He used to play on the stagecoaches, and his older brother Carl (famed stuntman) rode horses there. When asked how they knew each other, Paul responded, "Through the studios—all the cowboys knew each other." Cameron and his friends, the Pittis, Will Rogers, William S. Hart and Tom Mix, often relaxed at the stables. There were other connections as well. Bennie Pitti worked for Will Rogers. Will Rogers's father and Walter Cameron had been partners in Oklahoma years before.

INCE'S SECOND STUDIO

After Thomas Ince's alliance with D.W. Griffith and Mack Sennett went sour, he entered into a five-year lease agreement with Harry Culver for a new fourteen-acre studio fronting Washington Boulevard, east of the first studio.

One of the most recognizable studio images is the "mansion" administration building at the Thomas H. Ince Studios. It wasn't Tara, but it did appear in Selznick's photo image at the end of *Gone with the Wind*. Ince's office was located on the second floor, and many still feel or see his presence. *Courtesy of Bison Archives.*

It took two years to build the Thomas H. Ince Studio at 9336 Washington Boulevard. It was reminiscent of Mount Vernon, and a December 1, 1918 Los Angeles newspaper called it a "motion picture plant that looks like a beautiful Southern estate." The studio was planned by Meyer and Holler of the Milwaukee Building Company.

Ince, an actor-turned-producer and a visionary in the industry, promoted the glamour of moviemaking with a reverence. He entertained the king and queen of Belgium and President Woodrow Wilson. The administration building became a well-known landmark, and Ince was rapidly expanding his successful facility. In the early days, the studio fire chief also acted as the city fire chief. But in November 1924, amidst clouded circumstances, Thomas Harper Ince fell ill on William Randolph Hearst's yacht and reportedly died of a heart attack at home within the week. His wife, Elinor

K. Ince, once a talent agent, took the reins until the following year, when it became DeMille Studios.

Harry Culver spoke at the rededication, and Cecil B. DeMille became famous for his big-budget movies like *King of Kings*, which was the first movie shown at Grauman's Chinese Theatre. DeMille worked out a deal with Producers Distributing Corp. (PDC), and Cinema Corp. of America was formed as a holding company for PDC and DeMille Pictures Corp. Keith-Albee-Orpheum (KAO) purchased a half interest in PDC, and Radio Corp. of America bought in. Pathe Exchange Inc. merged with PDC/KAO/DeMille to become RKO in 1928. The name was changed to RKO-Pathe in 1930. Backlot acreage was added just south of the studio in 1931. Joseph Kennedy, who attempted to raise movies to an art form, had a financial interest in the studio during the Pathe years. Some of the stars working in those early years included Bette Davis, Robert Mitchum, Cary Grant, Carole Lombard, Katharine Hepburn, Fred Astaire and Ginger Rogers. *King Kong* was released in 1933, and those sets were later torched to make movie magic as "the burning of Atlanta" for *Gone with the Wind*. By 1935, the studio was known as Selznick International. David O. Selznick was the son-in-law of MGM studio chief Louis B. Mayer, which explains *Gone with the Wind*'s MGM release. *A Star Is Born*, *Intermezzo*, *Rebecca* and *Citizen Kane* also contributed to the studio's fame. Orson Welles and Alfred Hitchcock enjoyed great success on the lot. In the early '50s, even with Howard Hughes's backing, RKO went downhill.

The Desilu name appeared on the lawn about 1956, and for the next fifteen years, television was most important. The backlot provided locals with peeks at series like *The Untouchables*, *Hogan's Heroes*, *The Real McCoys* and *Lassie*. The studio was sold in 1968 to Perfect Film and Chemical and then to OSF Industries in 1969 to become Culver City Studios in 1970. In 1977, the studio became Laird International, a rental facility. When Laird filed for bankruptcy in 1986, Grant Tinker and Gannett (*USA Today*) paired to purchase the lot as GTG Entertainment. It became the Culver Studios. Sony Pictures Entertainment purchased the studio in 1991, and studio chief Jack Kindberg led a model renovation effort to render it a state-of-the-art facility. Culver City designated the "mansion" a historic landmark, and four bungalows were given "significant structure" status. It is also marked as a historic site. A 1994 ceremony on the front lawn marked the sale to PCCP Studio City Los Angeles. Although its famed forty-acre backlot is long gone, the front of the studios is one of the most recognizable photos to the world—a constant reminder of the importance of the movie industry to Culver City.

HAL ROACH STUDIOS

If zoning had not precluded expansion of producer Hal Roach's facilities in downtown Los Angeles, the Hal Roach Studios might never have relocated to Culver City. To find new studio space, Hal Roach called his friend Harry Culver and purchased his initial ten acres at $1,000 an acre. From 1919 to 1963, his "laugh factory to the world" was a proud fixture in town. That studio produced fifty comedies a year, as well as features. In a 1990 interview, ninety-eight-year-old Hal Roach said that Harold Lloyd was "the best comedian, second only to Chaplin" and the reason he could finance his new studio. He also offered fond memories of making Our Gang and Laurel and Hardy comedies. In addition to shooting on the studio lot, Roach filmed on location in Culver City. *Putting Pants on Philip* was the first teaming of Stan Laurel and Oliver Hardy. When you see it again, note the Culver Hotel and Main Street in the background. You will also recognize the Culver City Hall in their 1932 *County Hospital*. Culver City history was saved on film for posterity by Hal Roach productions. Laurel and Hardy's *The Music Box* won Roach his first Oscar in 1932, and the Our Gang comedy *Bored of Education* won another in 1936. Roach moved into television with series like *Topper*, *Amos and Andy*, *The Life of Riley*, *Trouble with Father* and *My Little Margie*. The Hal Roach Studio also produced the screen version of Steinbeck's *Of Mice and Men*. Hal Roach received an honorary Oscar in 1983 "in recognition of his unparalleled record of distinguished contributions to the motion picture art form."

During World War II, the Hal Roach Studio was known as "Fort Roach," where training films were made by Ronald Reagan, Alan Ladd and a multitude of other industry talents. Roach sold the studio in 1955 to his son Hal Jr., who eventually declared bankruptcy, and in 1963, the property was sold to become a part of the Landmark Industrial Tract. The Sons of the Desert placed a marker in the parkette at National and Washington Boulevards to commemorate this bastion of family entertainment.

SMALLER STUDIOS

In addition to the three major studios in Culver City, there were a number of small studios in town, including the Romayne Studios (northeast corner

Hal Roach was the third major studio built in Culver City and was known as the "laugh factory to the world." In 1992, Hal Roach was celebrated as the honorary chair of Culver City's seventy-fifth anniversary as he celebrated his 100th birthday.

The Our Gang comedies preserved Culver City history on film. The young actors were commonly seen shooting on location in Culver City.

of Ince and Washington) and Henry Lehrman Studios (area of Hal Roach Studios). Willat Studios, which made silent films, was located just off Washington Boulevard in the area of Willat Street. That studio was relocated to Beverly Hills, where it has stood since the 1920s as a private residence. It is known as the "Witch's House" due to its distinctive gingerbread character. In the 1990s, it almost found its way back to Culver City for use as a historic museum. Other small studios, such as Essenay on Venice and Cattaraugus, had Culver City mailing addresses but were just outside the city boundary.

THE HEART OF SCREENLAND

When Culver City adopted an official city seal in 1936, it read "The Heart of Screenland" to recognize the importance of the movie industry at the time. A thorn in the side of local residents, however, was the lack of recognition in movie credits. Movies made in Culver City either read "Made in Hollywood" or carried no city designation. *Citizen* publisher Eugene Donovan ran a contest in his newspaper in 1934 to rename the city. Entries included "Filmville" and "Cinema City," and the chamber of commerce later called for a drive to change the name to Hollywood. The chamber, proud of the city's movie heritage, actually adopted the slogan "Culver City, Where Hollywood Movies Are Made." Eventually, the Culver City and Hollywood Chambers of Commerce "buried the hatchet" in a ceremony at Grauman's Chinese Theatre in 1937. But it was not until 1991 that Sony Pictures Studio chief Arnie Shupack announced to the Culver City Council that movies made primarily in town (beginning with *Hook* and *Bugsy*) would read "Filmed in Culver City."

THE OSCARS

An Oscar is the Academy Award given for artistic distinction in filmmaking. The nickname of the coveted statuette can be traced back to the first decade of its existence. There are three people credited with the nickname, but many feel the most plausible originator was the librarian of the Academy of Motion Picture Arts and Sciences, Margaret Herrick, who suggested it looked like her Uncle Oscar. The Margaret Herrick Library is located on La Cienega Boulevard in Beverly Hills, and it is a wonderful resource.

The Oscar has particular relevance to Culver City history not only because the city is known as the "Heart of Screenland" but also because the statuette was designed by famed local art director Cedric Gibbons. Gibbons was MGM's art director in 1928, and his famous work has not been altered since, except for the higher pedestal in the 1940s. For accuracy's sake, it should be recognized that in the eighth decade of the Oscar, a new mold was made to facilitate the sharp image originally sculpted by George Stanley.

For "Oscar Party" enthusiasts, a little trivia is always helpful. Oscar is made of gold-plated britannium and stands thirteen and a half inches tall and weighs eight and a half pounds. The statuettes have been numbered since 1949, beginning with #501.

The Academy of Motion Picture Arts and Sciences was incorporated in May 1927, the same year that airmail pilot Charles A. Lindbergh made the first New York–Paris flight alone on his monoplane Spirit of St. Louis. The following year, Mary Pickford referred to the Academy as "the League of Nations" of the Motion Picture Industry.

The first Academy Awards ceremony was held on May 16, 1929, at 8:00 p.m. in the Blossom Room of the Hollywood Roosevelt Hotel. The first year, the awards were given in twelve categories. In 1934, a miniature statuette was awarded to six-year-old Shirley Temple, who made nine features that year.

After the initial awards event at the Hollywood Roosevelt, the ceremonies have been held at various locations through the years, including the Ambassador Hotel, the Biltmore Hotel, the Santa Monica Civic Auditorium, the Shrine Auditorium and the Kodak Theatre/Hollywood and Highland Center.

CHAPTER 5

EDUCATION

ELEMENTARY SCHOOLS

The old wooden structure that had housed La Ballona School since 1865 was deteriorating, and by the 1920s, plans were being made to replace it with a beautiful and roomier concrete school. Completed in 1926, the new school was set back from Washington Boulevard with a massive front lawn that was often used for May Day activities. The two-story structure had banisters at the end of the halls.

Bill Hahn, a 1937 graduate of La Ballona, is full of treasured memories. He lived on nearby Prospect Avenue and often went to school early to play tennis with friends on the school's courts. He remembers the playground surface, which was made of decomposed granite. The kindergarten was located on Matteson and Girard, where the children occasionally made things with hammers and wood. They had slides and swings, played marbles and spun tops for fun. Bill and his friends used to bring bread wrappers to school to wax the slides so they could go faster.

Although there was a cafeteria at La Ballona, Mr. Hahn remembers going home for lunch. His mother, like many others, was active in the PTA. Bill said his mom attended craft classes at school and made tie-dyed lampshades. He said the school "kept the neighborhood busy," even in the summertime.

La Ballona's library was situated on the second floor, where Los Angeles County had a branch at one time. Mrs. Boyd was the librarian when Bill

The second La Ballona School was a concrete structure that served locals until its demolition in the 1960s.

Hahn attended school. He also said that the school offered dental services for kids a couple of times a month and that his smallpox shot was also administered at school. His favorite teacher was Mrs. Magee, the orchestra and choir teacher. Bill Hahn and George Henderson were apparently the "spark plugs" who began to plan a 1984 La Ballona School reunion, during which they honored Mrs. Magee. Bill graduated in the school auditorium, and it is not surprising that his positive experiences as a student led him to become a teacher.

By the 1960s, Californians were acutely aware of earthquake preparedness. Local newspapers carried stories that showed peeling paint and broken windows at La Ballona. Poor maintenance gave it an aura of disrepair. The children's safety became the concern that pushed the PTA and other locals to advocate for the replacement of the school. The decision was made to demolish and replace La Ballona School, which sounded like it was ready to fall at any moment. The local school board put it out to bid. When it was time to demolish the old school, the contractor brought in the wrecking ball, but after a week, the unsafe building was not even dented.

When this "simple job" caused the demolition contractor to lose time and money, he went to the city for permission to use dynamite. Sam Cerra, known for his institutional memory, was working in the Culver City Engineering

Department at the time. He often related that the contractor wanted to blast the structure with explosives, but that went beyond state jurisdiction. The contractor had to go to city engineer Lou Molnar. Molnar reportedly refused the request for the use of dynamite due to its unstable nature, but he remembered that plastic explosives had been used in Korea because they offered better control. And that is what he authorized.

When the concrete school was demolished with the plastic explosives, the contractor found that the school walls were about eighteen inches thick with inch-thick steel rebar reinforcements. The irony, of course, was in the conclusion that the school would have withstood an earthquake after all.

The first two La Ballona Schools were a part of the Ballona School District, then Los Angeles Unified Schools. The current structure was completed in 1968, and La Ballona has been a part of Culver City Unified School District since the late 1940s, when the city became a charter city and the district became Culver City Unified School District.

Culver Grammar School was constructed in 1916, a year prior to the city's incorporation. The initial six classrooms were completed that year after a vote of 34–4, which passed a $55,000 bond issue to buy the property and build the school. Until 1920, when the board of supervisors made the change, Culver Grammar School was a part of the Palms school district.

In those early days, there was a flagpole in front of the school. Virgie Tinger (Eskridge) attended from kindergarten through eighth grade. She remembers the school day beginning with the blowing of a bugle and raising of the flag, which was followed by the Pledge of Allegiance. She also recalls the play equipment on Van Buren, which included swings with canvas seats and climbing bars. Back then, Braddock Drive cut through to Van Buren, and the school was situated with its back to Braddock, the front facing "School Street." School property behind and across the street served as a playground. In the 1950s, that space was surrounded by a chain-link fence with open gateways. During the day, Braddock was closed to allow for the children's safe passage across to the asphalt playground. Although the school gates were locked up after hours, the playground was open to the neighborhood kids and their families all week. Many children practiced basketball, softball and foursquare skills on that playground.

In a 1990 interview, retired Culver City educator Gladys Chandler related that the bank on the corner of Washington and Van Buren was hard pressed to give customers ten cents on the dollar during the Depression. The families suffered so greatly that the teachers at Culver Grammar, with the approval of

Once known as Culver City Grammar School, this school existed a year prior to the city's 1917 incorporation. It was rebuilt as the Linwood E. Howe School and today serves local children from kindergarten through fifth grade.

principal Bessie Brown, gave money out of their own checks for cafeteria food and clothes for the children. Gladys walked from her Lafayette Place home to teach at Culver Grammar starting in 1928. Virgie Eskridge spoke fondly of Gladys, her first grade teacher, and described her as a "kind, gentle, loving teacher." Gladys told some amusing stories too, like the day one child was tardy for school during Prohibition times. The child's excuse read that her father was making beer and it exploded, so she had to stay home and help clean up!

There was a separate kindergarten for the early Culver Grammar School. It was located in an old house on the school property. Children attended Culver Grammar through eighth grade, at which time they could matriculate to four-year high schools. Until Culver Junior and Senior High Schools opened their doors in the early 1950s, locals moved on to either Venice or Alexander Hamilton High School, depending on which side of Sepulveda their family resided.

Life in those times is often preserved through local media. On the front page of a 1940 newspaper, there was notice of a contest to name the school newspaper, with a prize of one dollar. The winner was Jo Anne Stevenson's *What Goes On.* On the second page, one of the headlines was "Improvements." That article began, "The people in Studio Village will no longer bump into things at night! The city is planning to install street lights soon." The coverage offered a broad scope of articles. One eye-catcher on page four was the Hobby Column. "Pleasant pastimes" were listed as "making soap, carvings, paintings, model ships and airplanes," as well as collecting "first edition books, rare stamps, and unique what-nots." Student Charles Rozaire was singled out for his hobby of writing to people in different countries, while Freddy Simpson collected badges and pins. (Charles became Dr. Rozaire, a noted archaeologist/anthropologist.) Charleen Reeds collected pictures of movie stars, including her reported favorites Clark Gable and Myrna Loy. The "Spring Fashions" column's target readership was seventh and eighth graders. One popular outfit for girls consisted of "a full Russian striped blouse with a plain colored skirt. The finishing touches are a pan scrubber beanie, bobby socks, new style wedge-heel coolies and a strand of bubble beads." There were even instructions for pan scrubber beanies that promised to "give you an outstanding personality." A story titled "The Mystery of the Haunted House" by Bathon Hafen on page five left readers hanging until next month. The editor also promised upcoming columns like "Radio News and Madame Puzzlewits."

Since we learn a lot from history and its repetitive nature, the following advice to parents seemed especially pertinent. It appeared on the back of a 1936 report card.

Reasons Parents Should Visit Schools

- To keep in touch with the work of their children.
- To encourage their teachers.
- To get firsthand information about the work of the schools.
- To become acquainted personally with the teacher and principal.
- To learn at firsthand the condition under which their children work.
- To learn the problems the children must meet.
- To make it possible for the school officials to interpret to parents the policies under which the school operates.
- To aid in developing real school spirit in the community.

What to Observe

- Sanitary condition of the school building.
- The general discipline and management of the school.
- The attitude of the teacher toward the children.
- The attitude of the children toward the teacher.
- The size of the classes.
- The physical conditions under which the teacher and pupils work.
- Facilities offered for the development of health.
- To what extent their own children participate in the school's activities.
- The equipment of the school.

Madelyn Needham Hahn lived on Wesley Street and made friends at Culver Grammar with other girls like Virgie Tinger and Caroline Halverson. She came to Culver Grammar in eighth grade and recalls the importance of penmanship, math flash cards, the Halloween carnival and their "clever and funny" class play called *Aboard a Slow Train in Mizzoury*. Madelyn recalls that gum chewing was not well received. She shared a poem that her sister Phyllis (class of 1943) saved from her teacher, a Mrs. Catlin, who made her point in verse:

> *A gum-chewing girl*
> *And a cud-chewing cow*
> *Are very alike*
> *But different somehow*
> *What was the difference?*
> *Oh, I know now*
> *It's the thoughtful look*
> *On the face of the cow!*

In later days, there was a principal of Culver Grammar named Mr. Howe. When the new elementary school opened in 1968, it was dedicated in honor of Linwood E. Howe. At the time, the school board was composed of Alvin H. Weissman, president; Mrs. Jeanette Carl, vice-president; J. Paul Spector, clerk; and members Mrs. Edna Larkin and Dr. William E. Vickery.

Earl Patton served as superintendent. On the 1969 dedication plaque at the entrance of Linwood E. Howe School, Mr. Howe was described as "a man who identified himself with children and who was sensitive to their needs and feelings. A man whose gifts to those he touched were enthusiasm, vitality and purposefulness." And the only question to answer now is, "What does the E stand for in Linwood E. Howe?" Elmer—and that was verified by his son of the same name!

CULVER CITY UNIFIED SCHOOL DISTRICT: SECONDARY SCHOOLS

Let's take a step back to understand the process that led to Culver City becoming a unified school district. After the 1915 annexation of Palms to Los Angeles, the area destined to become Culver City became a school district without a school, as La Ballona School had been a part of Palms. In 1920, three years after Culver City's incorporation, the Palms School District was changed to Culver, which was 3.22 square miles serving a population of seven hundred.

In 1916, Culver City Grammar School became a reality with the passage of a $55,000 bond issue and a 34–4 vote. That election took place prior to the city's incorporation and prior to women's suffrage, hence the small number of votes cast.

Washington School, on McManus Street, was constructed in 1925. Although it suffered earthquake damage in 1933, it was subsequently remodeled to meet earthquake standards and is still in use today. Culver and Washington Schools were the only two schools in the Culver City School District for many years. During those early years, elementary school was attended through eighth grade. Secondary students from Culver City attended Palms Junior High and then Venice High School or Alexander Hamilton High School, depending on which side of Sepulveda their families resided.

The 1947 vote by Culver City residents to become a charter city rearranged the district boundaries to coincide with the city boundaries. That brought Betsy Ross, Farragut and La Ballona schools into our district. Shortly thereafter, interest in building the city's own secondary schools passed a ballot measure in January 1949. Plans for junior and senior high school were then realized in 1950.

In 1952, shortly after the Culver Crest area was annexed to Culver City, El Rincon School was built on land donated by developer R.J. Blanco, who also donated the adjacent land to be used as a park in perpetuity. Blanco Park is used by El Rincon School as part of its playground during the day and is an excellent example of the benefit of the joint powers agreement between the city and the school district. El Marino Elementary School opened in 1952 as well. The school had to be closed due to declining enrollment but was reopened in 1994 as a language magnet. Culver City has been a pioneer in the language immersion field. Culver City began the first Spanish Immersion Program in the country in 1971 at Linwood E. Howe Elementary School and later established a Japanese Immersion Program in 1991 at Farragut School. Linda Vista School was built in Blair Hills in 1959.

At its peak, there were eight operating elementary schools in Culver City: La Ballona, Culver Grammar, Washington School, Betsy Ross, Farragut School, El Rincon School, Linda Vista and El Marino School. Linda Vista, in Blair Hills, was leased for some time and later sold, and two (the former Washington and Betsy Ross schools) are now on long-term leases due to declining enrollment. El Marino School was also closed but reopened as a language magnet in 1994. Today, there are five operating elementary schools in the district.

The motivation for Culver City to become a charter city in 1947 was in the interest of local control. The move to become a unified school district was an extension of that thinking. Locals saw their property tax dollars siphoned outside to support nearby schools with very limited impact on local education. Once local property taxes supported local schools, Culver City Unified earned a reputation as a "lighthouse district"—a leader in education.

The Tenth Amendment to the U.S. Constitution reserves states' rights in education, and the state constitution, the California Education Code and state laws empower and obligate local boards to provide for free and equal education. This explains the requirement for the state architect to approve plans for schools and why the county runs school board elections. School district facilities, as used for public schools, are not subject to the authority of local government. In Culver City, however, there is a negotiated joint powers agreement and a city/school district liaison committee that effects cooperation between both governing bodies.

Like many other states, California funded education, but by 1968, things began to change. Nine parents joined John Serrano to file suit against multiple state and local officials, charging that this system of financing resulted in an unfair and unequal education for their children. By 1971, the California Supreme Court determined the system discriminated against poorer neighborhoods. The Serrano-Priest decision in 1976 completed the mandate to eradicate unequal funding in California. School funding changed in 1978, as the Jarvis-Gann Initiative (Proposition 13) passed. It seriously impacted state and local funding by limiting and rolling back property taxes. By 1983, the state's expenditures had exceeded annual revenues by $1 billion a year, obliterating the surpluses.

After Bill Honig became state superintendent of schools, the 1982–83 legislature committed to reform K–12 education. The result was the Hughes-Hart Educational Reform Act of 1983. The bill reformed graduation standards and salaries of beginning teachers and revised school financing. It also gave boards of education the major responsibility of preparing, adopting and implementing school district budgets. What did this mean locally? Former board member Steve Schwartz recalls agonizing budget cuts after Prop. 13. Fine arts were eliminated, and reduced funding yielded a proliferation of supportive nonprofit, business, city and individual partnerships. The first was the formation of the Culver City Education Foundation in 1981. A 1970s contract with the Culver City Redevelopment Agency designed to reduce impacts of the student influx from new housing developments (old MGM backlots) was nullified. A new agreement in the 1990s provided $2.2 million for capital improvements and reinstated annual entitlements, with 25 percent going only to capital improvements. Later, the overwhelming passage of Measure T was the next response to need. Overall, Culver City consistently supports its schools as a high priority. However, since the Culver City Redevelopment Agency was collapsed in 2012, it comes with serious impacts to Culver City schools as well.

Board members are elected at large in odd-numbered years. In 1947, the *Evening Star-News* reported, "They meet at least once a month to take care of school problems and serve without pay." Today, the board meets the first and third Tuesdays of each month, and members receive a small stipend. Some never even miss a meeting! The charge is policy, and the board's only employee is the superintendent, who is the educational leader of the district. Board members all have different styles, visibility and challenges. For many, the challenge was Prop 13. For Edna Larkin, it was the Robert Frost Auditorium. But for many others, it was the controversy surrounding the opening or closing of schools, perhaps the closing of the high school at lunch, closing the natatorium, opening of the youth health center, annexation of Fox Hills to the district or strategic planning. A shared frustration takes the form of state-mandated programs that pass the legislature without the necessary funding. And according to one insightful former board member, "In those times, no one wants to hear the facts."

The early board of trustees of the Culver School District numbered three, but it increased to a five-member board of education after the city charter was adopted. In a special August 1947 edition of the *Evening Star-News*, front-page headlines read, "Culver City Is Film Capital of World." The second section read, "Charter Voted This Year for Culver City," while a third section was devoted entirely to becoming a unified school district. The paper described the charter action as an end to a long campaign over "several years of agitation." There were also articles on all five principals of the elementary schools in Culver City at that time. Some of their names may be familiar: Mrs. Gladys Chandler (Washington), Louis Tallman (Culver Grammar School), Milfred Schafer (La Ballona), Donald Piety (Betsy Ross) and Robert Kelley (Farragut). Who was on that board of education? Mayo D. Wright, Ed Castle, Robert Ford, Monte Hover and Mrs. Ellen Nix.

The construction of a district office, junior high and a three-year high school began in 1950. In 1953, the first Culver High graduating class was called the Titans, and the student body adopted the centaur as the school mascot. The first graduating class, numbering fewer than 150, gave a painting of a centaur as its class gift to the new high school. It was located high on the first gym building.

But what is the significance of the centaur? According to *Bullfinch's Mythology: The Age of Fable*, centaurs were "monsters" that had the head and torso of a man but the bottom half of a horse. Ancients held horses in high esteem, so this "union" was created with good character traits. We might also speculate that the centaur was chosen because one of these creatures, Chiron, who was instructed by Apollo and Diana, was known for his skill in medicine, hunting, music and the art of prophecy. The honor society at Culver City High School took on the name of Chirons.

In an interview with Pat Martin Clapp, a 1954 Culver High graduate, Clapp notes that mascots were especially important at school athletic events. So Pat, a seamstress even then, designed a costume for a "manned" centaur (Wencil Jansta and Robert Hoskins) to proudly trot around the football field during games to arouse school spirit. History repeated itself during the homecoming game of 1993, as the student league stressed early traditions. A committee worked with Pat to redesign an updated centaur, with Justin Ross and Henry Sebata manning the mythological character. When asked about her interpretation of the centaur, former mayor Jozelle Lawless Smith, a Culver High graduate, pointed to the brains of a man and the strength of the horse. And so you have it—the best of both worlds.

Culver City High School proudly shows off its centaur mascot at the school's entrance. After the 1949 election that made Culver a unified school district, the junior and senior high schools were built next to each other on Elenda Street. The high school also boasts an Academy of Visual and Performing Arts.

Originally, the junior and senior high schools shared front doors on Elenda Street. Both were three-year schools. The first class graduated from Culver High in 1953. The dedication in the 1953 yearbook, the *Olympian*, read:

> *Dedicated to them...*
> *To the first time they walked down the corridors*
> *Until the last time they walked out...*
> *And all the other days.*
> *The day they first went to a high school dance...*
> *The day they organized their clubs*
> *And became the first members...*
> *Elected their first officers...*
> *Planned their first high school activities.*
> *They were the first class in,*
> *The first class out.*
> *—The Titans, class of '53*

Turning the pages of the yearbook is like peeling back layers of time. There were pictures of the staff, headed by principal John Plank, and familiar names like Mrs. Ruby Shipp, Mr. Ed Helwick, Mr. Del Goodyear and school nurse Mrs. Anna Marie Allard. The formality of the times was apparent in shots of the "Snowball" dance in December, the Girls League Installations, Aristonians, National Honor Society, Chirons, Future Business Leaders of America, Coordinating Council and Key Club. The Junior Red Cross showed commitment, and a Cadet Corps is pictured getting ready to advance the colors at a home football game.

TITAN DUANE KENNEDY'S WORDS FROM THE FIRST YEARBOOK:

The land was barren not long ago.
Then the builders came.
Man's plans for the future began.
The angles of wood, planes of glass,
Curves of steel pillars of brick...
All intermingled
Like the different lives they'll be a part of.
The rugged skyline of a sturdy school
Blessed with the touch of the modern artist's hands
Created to deal with modern problems...
Modern people.
It took awhile and it's still not done,
But now the land is fertile,
Producing every day a better youth.

Activists like parent Bessie Freiden spearheaded fundraisers for lights at the high school stadium, Helms Field. Robert Frost Auditorium opened in 1964 and is scheduled for its second renovation in 2013. A natatorium, in a district/city partnership, subsequently opened but had to be closed in the 1990s for budgetary reasons.

In 1979, Sunrise High School (Culver Park since 1987) opened at the El Marino site as an alternative school for students. In 2012, Culver Park moved to the current secondary site in upscale bungalows. Grade levels were readjusted in 1983 to make elementary schools K–5, the junior high became a middle school and Culver High is now a four-year high school. This explains some of the space issues the district regularly faces.

The Culver City Unified School District's Language Immersion programs continue to thrive.

In the 1980s, the district, in partnership with UCLA, established a Youth Heath Center, and the commitment to lifelong learning is apparent with a very active Culver City Adult School. In addition to the PTAs at each school, other support groups—Culver City Education Foundation, Advocates for Language Learning, Friends of the Youth Health Center, booster clubs, etc.—were established as school funding changed with Prop 13.

In addition to hosting highly regarded public schools and pre-schools, several well-known private schools have relocated to Culver City. The area of the Hayden and Landmark Industrial tracts has drawn schools like Willows Community School, Turning Point School and Park Century School. Long-term leases of CCUSD property include the Echo Horizon School (former Washington School) and Wildwood School (former Betsy Ross School).

CHAPTER 6

ENTERTAINMENT, CULTURAL RESOURCES AND MORE LASTING MEMORIES

NIGHTCLUBS

Culver City was in its infancy when the Volstead Act brought Prohibition in 1919. The city, incorporated just two years prior, was rapidly becoming the "Heart of Screenland," with three major studios situated along Washington Boulevard. There were also several small studios like the architecturally distinct Willat Studio. Culver City was fertile ground for the entertainment of the movie crowd as well as the locals.

Perhaps the best-known nightclub was Frank Sebastian's Cotton Club, which was originally the Green Mill. Sebastian was already experienced in the entertainment business before he came to Culver City. In his book *Out With the Stars: Hollywood Nightlife in the Golden Era,* historian Jim Heimann mentions the already successful Sebastian's Cafe on Windward Avenue in Venice. Sebastian's customers enjoyed "Las Vegas–type" acts at his Cotton Club on Washington Boulevard at National, which offered valet parking, three dance floors and full orchestras, rivaling the club of the same name in New York. Louis Armstrong played at Sebastian's Cotton Club and actually lived on Wade Street in Culver City in the 1920s. Early residents Clarita Marquez Young and Charles R. Lugo identified the house years ago, and owners Mary and James O'Neill cooperated with the Historic Preservation Advisory Committee when they furnished county records showing Armstrong as its first owner in 1923.

Frank Sebastian's Cotton Club was one of the most celebrated of Culver City's nightclubs. Its ads drew people to hear some of the best musicians in the business, including Louis Armstrong.

In the April 7, 1999 edition of the *International Herald Tribune*, there was a fascinating interview with Lionel Hampton, who had just concluded a week playing drums in the Meridien Hotel at Porte Maillot. In the article, Hampton acknowledged that he started out at the age of eighteen in 1926 at the Cotton Club in Culver City with Les Hite. Hampton remembered Sebastian being tired of his old band after a few years, so he brought in Louis Armstrong to front Les Hite. Hampton recalled Sebastian's introduction of Armstrong and Hampton as the "world's greatest trumpet player, Louis Armstrong, with the world's fastest drummer, Lionel Hampton."

Other than the Cotton Club, Roscoe "Fatty" Arbuckle's Plantation Cafe was probably the next best-known night spot in Culver City. Arbuckle established his nightclub on Washington Boulevard across from La Ballona School. The name of the club was spelled out in flowers in its heyday. According to local lore, the cafe was built by resident/contractor Dan Coombs in just twenty-eight days.

Who was Fatty Arbuckle? Roscoe Arbuckle was a comic actor, director and screenwriter born in Smith Center, Kansas, in 1887. He began his career as a plumber's assistant, after which he transitioned into performing in carnivals and vaudeville shows. In Ephraim Katz's *Film Encyclopedia*, Arbuckle is referred to as "baby-faced and amazingly agile for his heavy frame," which was reported to be over three hundred pounds. His film career began as an extra in 1908. In 1913, Arbuckle joined Mack Sennett's "Keystone Kops," which led to a series of short comedies with stars like Charlie Chaplin. Arbuckle's screenwriting and directing began in 1916, and the following year, he formed his own production company, which gave Buster Keaton his start. Keaton later made movies in Culver City's studios.

In 1921, at the height of his popularity, Arbuckle's career was destroyed by scandal. A young actress, Virginia Rappe, died after being raped at a wild party given by Arbuckle at the St. Francis Hotel in San Francisco. Arbuckle was charged with the young woman's assault. After two hung juries, a third trial ended in the actor's acquittal, but his film career was permanently damaged.

Arbuckle opened the Plantation Cafe in 1928 with design help from MGM's noted art director Cedric Gibbons. On opening night, Fatty Arbuckle performed a comedy routine for his peers in the film world, which included Charlie Chaplin, Buster Keaton, Mary Pickford, Douglas Fairbanks and Tom Mix. The Plantation Cafe went under with the crash of the stock market. Fatty Arbuckle died in 1933 at the age of forty-six, never able to accomplish his planned comeback.

There were many other nightclubs in Culver City, most of them located along Washington Boulevard. The Green Mill, King's Tropical Inn (5935 Washington), the Hot Spot Cafe (near the creek), Barton's, Ford's Castle, Moonlite Gardens, the Hoosegow, Casa Mañana and Frank's Bar and Grill (across from RKO) were all very popular. Kirk Kerkorian's parents owned a bar at the East End on Adams. Kerkorian and his boxing champ brother "Nish" fought frequently at Sy Saenz's Boxing Arena. Two sisters, Gladys and "Babe," who were married to local firemen, owned the Hot Spot at one time. It was known as Gladys's Hot Spot, where mobster Mickey Cohen was spotted on occasion.

Culver City's irregular boundaries also made Washington Boulevard an attractive location for nightclubs, but not for reasons you would anticipate. If you look at the map of the city, you will notice that all of Culver City is south of Venice Boulevard but that the boundaries weave in and out from Washington. Although the total area of the city has never been more than five square miles, it encompasses a seven-mile stretch of West Washington Boulevard. Years ago, retired city treasurer Lu Herrera shared that in early times, the jurisdiction of a business was often determined by the placement of the cash register. Some establishments put their cash registers on wheels. When noisy, rowdy behavior resulted in a call to the police, the cash register was simply rolled to the Los Angeles side or vice versa.

The King's Tropical Inn is pictured in its second structure on Washington Boulevard at La Cienega. Although it had long ceased operation as a nightclub, it was the only example of Byzantine architecture in Culver City before the Northridge earthquake destroyed it in 1994.

But how did one acquire alcohol during Prohibition? Early residents still remember a man named Max, who drove in his big Cadillac from Malibu to Santa Monica with five-gallon cans of pure alcohol. Local bootleggers like "Benny" and "Lucky" diluted it with distilled water and added oak chips (so they could say it was "aged in oak") and caramel coloring before bottling and selling it. Some relate that the office of the boxing arena was used to sell the bootlegged spirits. To complete the picture, there were "bookie joints" all over, too. The "Auto Dealers Club" was just one, reputedly owned by Chicago gamblers.

During the 1920s and '30s, Culver City earned its tawdry reputation for nightclubs, bootlegging and gambling. Although many find it embarrassing, let's not rewrite history but simply put it in the context of the times.

THEATERS IN CULVER CITY, THE HEART OF SCREENLAND

When Harry Culver built his Hotel Hunt in the early 1920s, the building site had to be cleared. The city offices moved down the street to Van Buren Place. The theater, renamed the Meralta Theatre, moved into a new structure on the 9600 block of Culver Boulevard. Will Rogers acted as the master of ceremonies for the grand opening, while filmmaker Thomas Ince provided the movie, *The Galloping Fish*.

The Meralta shared the block with Western Union, Southern California Water Co., Pulone's Sweet Shop, the Edison Co., Holland's Draperies, attorney R.H. Coombs, Mayo D. Wright Insurance and the Blaine-Walker Building, which housed the early courthouse. The new name was a portmanteau of the surnames of owners Pearl Merrill and Laura Peralta, who lived above the plush new theater. It appears, from old directories, that Merrill also had a real estate office and later an insurance office, first on Irving Place and then on Culver next to the theater. In a 1990 interview, retired principal Gladys Chandler described Pearl Merrill, who served on the board of education, as "forceful, positive, with a big heart." She told of Merrill's commitment, which sent her traveling all over the country at her own expense to interview teachers.

A 1932 Culver City Woman's Club scrapbook pictured Laura Peralta as president of the club, whose roster of 131 members read like a who's who of Culver City. Peralta's installation was in June 1932 in the gardens of the Woman's Club at 3835 Watseka Avenue. The luncheon speaker was listed as "a noted lecturer…on two continents, who teaches the secret yogi methods of breathing exercises." Peralta's term was filled with teas, musical performances, plays and philanthropy. The cost of elaborate luncheon meetings and bridge teas was just thirty-five cents. The traditional president's scrapbook offered personal insight into Peralta. Peralta's mother, Isabell O. Peralta, was an Otero whose family arrived in California in 1850, reportedly from Spain. She was baptized at the church on the Los Angeles Plaza in 1867. It seems that Laura was one of nine children. Another daughter married Manuel Saenz, whose family has a long history in this area.

The most interesting find was an article that told how Merrill and Peralta "gave up careers as a popular stage comedy team and came to Culver City as pioneer operators and managers of the Meralta Theatre on the site of the Culver Hotel." It also cited the theater as an impromptu rendezvous for famous players and directors like Charley Chase, the original Hal Roach "Our Gang," Keystone Kops and Western Stars.

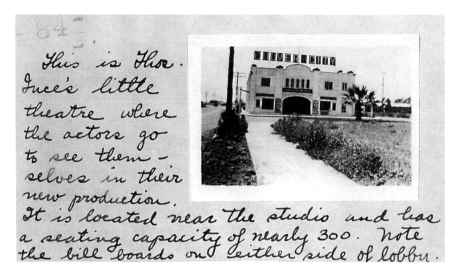

This is Thos. Ince's little theatre where the actors go to see themselves in their new production. It is located near the studio and has a seating capacity of nearly 300. Note the bill boards on either side of lobby.

This 1918 scrapbook page depicts the first theater in Culver City, in which the city rented its first offices on the second floor. A family recorded their trip to Culver City with notes that Ince's actors went to see themselves at this three-hundred-seat movie theater. *Courtesy of Todd Spiegelberg.*

Filming on location in Culver City is commonplace, even at the entrance to a theater. The Meralta Theatre was popular with all age groups. In addition to the snack bar inside, there was also a Meralta Sweet Shop next door run by the Pulone family. *Courtesy of Bison Archives.*

The Culver Theatre opened in 1947. Designated with city landmark status under the city's historic preservation ordinance in 1991, it has become a Center Theatre Group (CTG) performing arts facility, the Kirk Douglas Theatre. The Culver City Council gave CTG permission to remove and restore the Culver Script for use nearby.

During World War II, the Meralta Theatre caught fire. With a wartime moratorium on the building, the city allowed the theater to relocate temporarily to the second-floor auditorium of city hall (corner of Culver and Duquesne). The projection booth remained until city hall was demolished to make way for the new city hall, which opened in 1995. The rebuilt Meralta Theatre operated for many years. In 1983, the Meralta Plaza was constructed as a redevelopment project on the same block as the Meralta Theatre.

The Culver Theater, designed by Carl G. Moeller, began construction in 1945. Built in the (Skouras-ized) Moderne style with 1,160 seats, it opened on August 13, 1947, with a showing of *The Red Stallion*. The original cost was $175,000, but the value at its opening was estimated at $225,000, which included equipment. The first manager was Ted Morris.

"Culver City, the Heart of Screenland" has appeared on the city seal since 1936, a reflection of the importance of three major studios and other entertainment-related businesses in the city. At the end of World War II, people in Culver City were delighted with the construction of a second movie theater. "The Culver" spelled entertainment in neon and offered job opportunities for local youth. The ushers and usherettes were uniformed in white shirts, black bow ties, red jackets and gray pants with silver stripes. They took direction from their tuxedo-clad managers. "Sneak Previews" were common benefits, and movie stars like Ann-Margret and Elvis occasionally slipped in to see movies. This local landmark remains a symbol of city founder Harry Culver's interest in the industry that provided the economic base for Culver City.

As the need for single theaters and ushers declined, the theater was sold and reconfigured into a triplex. It was subsequently operated by Fox West Coast Theatres, National General, Mann Theatre Corporation and Great Western Theatres, with the last owner being the Culver City Redevelopment Agency in 1989. The last movie shown at the theater was the Eddie Murphy hit *Coming to America*.

The Center Theatre Group signed a sixty-year lease with the Culver City Redevelopment Agency to turn the Culver into a performing arts space as the Kirk Douglas Theatre, which opened in October 2004.

Just to clarify, the Mann Theater, which was located nearby on Washington Boulevard at Dunn Drive, is actually in the city of Los Angeles, so for some time, the "Heart of Screenland" was actually without a theater until the new entertainment complex was built in Downtown Culver City.

Culver City's own Studio Drive-In opened in 1948, closed in 1993 and was demolished in 1998. That property became the new home of the Kayne-Eras Center and fifty-seven single-family homes.

For many, the memories of the drive-in began with family outings. Parents took the opportunity to get little ones into their "jammies" and head to the drive-in for family movies. Food treats took the form of popcorn, candy and, sometimes, homemade sweets. Oftentimes, parents turned to check out a quiet back seat halfway through the movie only to discover sweet, slumbering children.

By the time high school came around, parents were not as excited to send their children to the drive-in on dates, and there seemed to be an abundance of rules in hopes that they would actually see the movies. Culverite Alan Rowe still remembers packing the trunk of his '53 Chevy with friends and "the excitement of pulling it off and the fear of getting caught." Others admit slipping through the fences to meet friends. Cathy Duncan Lugo remembers her parents taking her. She loved the play equipment by the snack

The Studio Drive-In is pictured in the upper right quadrant, between Sepulveda (left) and Jefferson (right) Boulevards. This early 1950s photograph shows the small golf course and range lower right (Lugo Ranch property) edged by Sawtelle Boulevard.

bar, particularly the swings, and "the giant picture—it was really fun." She even knew what she wore: a shorts outfit and her red Keds tennis shoes. She also mentioned taking walks with her mom along the creek and sneaking into the drive-in during the day to play on the swings. Carlos Lugo, her husband, shared memories of relaxing in his pajamas in the back seat of the family's '55 Ford station wagon. The first movie he saw was "a Disney," and on his last trip, he took his older daughter to see *Naked Gun*.

Jozelle Smith contributed, "I remember as a senior at Culver High… my girlfriend and I once smuggled our 'little sisters' [sophomores] in, one covered with blankets in the back seat and one in the trunk! How could we have done that?! I remember giggling a lot." Steve Rose was direct and to the point when he recalls his "mom's '61 Chevy and a girl by the name of Judy…I do not remember the movie!"

Steve Newton noted, "A lot of those memories should be kept to ourselves—like the saying 'What happens in Vegas stays in Vegas.' The

Studio Drive-In was referred to as the 'Passion Pit' in the early '60s. We would unload the surfboards from my Woody wagon and sweep the sand off of the mattress in the back." He related that surfers generally replaced the two rear seats in their Woodies with old mattresses in the back so they could carry more people and surfboards to the beach. This made a great cruising/party wagon. Steve added, "I believe I set the record for being busted by the Culver City police for drinking beer at the drive-in with twelve people in the Woody. Sue won't let me tell any of the other stories."

When Cathy and George Zermeno moved to the city in 1954, she remembers that "everyone was spending money on their homes and could not spend too much going to the movies with the family, so the drive-in theater was the greatest thing!" Robbin Smith recalls:

> *I think I went to the Studio Drive-In more times in the trunk of a car than in the cockpit. The good part was not having to pay—the bad was that those up front would crank up the "rear" speakers, which were located about where your head was when stuffed in the trunk with another couple. By the time they let us out at the rear of the lot to get back in the cab, we were nearly deaf. Later, Sharon and I would attend in my red 1950 Chevy panel truck, park backwards with the rear door open and view the movie in the comfort of a Philippine mahogany–paneled and carpeted tool shop. I guess it wasn't all bad—we're still married after forty-plus years!*

Ruby Elbogen remembered "piling as many friends as we could into a car—including the trunk—to save money. We hooked the speaker onto the window and laughed through the entire movie. When I went with a special boy, it was another story altogether." Like so many, her high school memories transition to family outings with their kids in pajamas and Dinah's chicken.

Culver High grad Susan Riss went to the Studio Drive-In with dates but clarified, "Of course I was such a goodie-two-shoes. I think I was the only girl in the place who saw every minute of the movie!" She shared fond times spent "with my aunt and uncle in the front seat and all us cousins in the back giggling all through the movie." They often got lost returning from the snack bar or bathroom since all the cars looked alike.

Racetracks

The first of two tracks in Culver City was situated on the present-day site of Carlson Park. It appears that the track first opened as a horse-racing track in 1923. That only lasted about a year, and on December 14, 1924, it reopened as a board-racing track simply called the Speedway. It was very well known, but much of the written information on it refers to it as the Los Angeles Speedway. The track was moved from Beverly Hills.

In September 1924, the city accepted land for public street purposes from Gilbert H. Beesmyer of the Speedway Corp. Later that year, Resolution #600 was adopted on December 15 to commend "Capt. Cain and officers of CCPD for the efficient manner at which crowds at auto races held December 14 were handled." The record also reflected that more than fifty thousand visitors were in attendance that opening day. News coverage relayed that Bonnie Hill took top honors by averaging 126.9 miles per hour in the "Indy-type" races. Barney Oldfield also raced at our Speedway. Although the Speedway lasted longer than the horse-racing track, just a few years later, the portion of the property bounded by Braddock (between Le Bourget and Motor Avenue) was considered for the first park in Culver City. The trustees passed Resolution #1343 on August 8, 1927, which approved and ratified the action of the City Parks Board and Art Commission in selecting the name Victory Park.

The second Culver City track was located at the western edge of the city on Washington Boulevard. Originally, it was built for greyhound races. Many speculate that west end annexation in the mid-1920s intended to include the revenue from its pari-mutuel betting. But according to city records, it was not until March 8, 1932, that the Culver City Kennel Club was granted a permit and license for "canine racing, coursing with canine sales and exhibits." The location was listed as 13455 Washington Boulevard.

State anti-gambling legislation closed the track, but February 8, 1935, headlines in the *Citizen* newspaper read, "Dog Racing Bill Pondered." It reported that the reopening of the Culver City Dog Racetrack was a possibility because a bill introduced by Assemblyman Malone would legalize dog racing in California. It also stated that the track had been closed for two years. The March 22 edition of the same paper reported that the assembly took action to permit it again.

This track location was also the home of midget auto races in the 1940s. Fred Machado built his own car, which was normally driven by Ken Stansbury. One day, Stansbury failed to show, so Indianapolis driver

Culver City's western boundary has been located just before Lincoln Boulevard since the 1920s. Although many cite the early greyhound and car races as the motivation for the unusual finger-shape protruding into Los Angeles, it was probably intended to include both sides of Washington Boulevard, a busy commercial street that ran from downtown Los Angeles to Abbot Kinney's Venice of America. *Courtesy of Fred Machado.*

Dempsey Wilson took the wheel. Local businessman George Newnam had his midget debut there in 1950. In a 1990 interview, Mr. Newnam related that the track was later used for jalopies and was a "motocross speedway." He also explained that it was originally a quarter-mile banked asphalt track but was later doubled to make it a figure eight. This was verified by the city engineering department in the form of a 1953 aerial photo of the track. City records show the last car entry as Auction City. Many will remember Dick Lane advertising jalopies as "old leatherbritches" on Channel 5.

CULVER CITY AIRPORT: THE EARLY YEARS

The Culver City Airport was located between Sepulveda Boulevard and Mesmer, edged by Jefferson Boulevard. It had its beginnings in 1927 and was originally known as the Baker Airport. The first owners were Frank Baker and Bob Blair. According to a 1973 publication of *Los Angeles Aeronautics* written by Northrop Institute professor D.D. Hatfield, the airport was L shaped, with runways in two directions. Its first planes were listed as a Waco 10, an OX-5 Jenny and a Hispano Suiza–powered Ryan M-1. Later, when it housed a dealership for the Buhl Aircraft Company's planes, it became Buhl Pacific

Culver City Airport existed from the 1920s through the 1940s. As head of the National Real Estate Association, Harry Culver (center) flew his Stinson Detroiter from the little airport with his pilot and family across the country in 1929. He spoke at six hundred different stops. The airport, located at Jefferson and Sepulveda, was eventually annexed from Los Angeles County. *Courtesy of the Culver family.*

Aircraft Company and was managed by Bob Blair. Mrs. Margaret Blair was a flyer, and she was reportedly active in the flight operations, which included flight instruction and passenger and charter flights.

On the back of Hatfield's book, Don Wiggins wrote, "In the Roaring Twenties, Los Angeles meant Hollywood, that crazy movie town where more stunt pilots were employed than on the nation's fledgling airlines—where studio bosses like Syd Chaplin and Cecil B. De Mille flew their own crates." According to Hatfield, the Blair school taught many notables, including Clark Gable, James Stewart, Ruth Chatterton and Henry Fonda.

The Buhl Company and the airport were sold in October 1928 to Flying Incorporated, owned by formal naval aviator William G. McAdoo Jr.; W.E. McManus Jr., formerly with the Royal Air Force; and a San Francisco aviator by the name of Lansing Pedis. Their chief pilot was Harry Ashe.

A search through city records shows that a resolution was read before the board of trustees on June 19, 1929. It was from the chamber of commerce "advocating and endorsing a municipally owned, operated and controlled airport and requesting the Board of Trustees of the City of Culver City to take necessary steps to acquire a site for the same." Two months later, after a feasibility study that showed that an operation at that time could not be profitably operated, the city dispensed with further discussion.

Eventually, this airport was named the Culver City Airport, and city founder Harry Culver, who purchased a plane in 1928, flew out of it. During the 1930s, there were no annexations to the city, so although it was called the Culver City Airport, it was not actually within the city limits. It had a Culver City mailing address, as did the property to the west where Hughes built the Spruce Goose and became a major employer of Culver City residents in the 1940s. Hughes had an airport as well. It was listed in the 1950 U.S. Geological Survey map as "industrial airport."

The Culver City Airport was a progressive little airport, with numerous female pilots and a Goodyear blimp. A young local named Jean Kleopfer (Barker) took flying lessons there at the age of sixteen. She still laughs about the time in early 1941 when she paid eight dollars for a lesson. Pete Leaman was the operator/manager of the airport then. When this well-known instructor taught her to fly, he asked her if she had ever "dropped her cookies" as he prepared her to land through the utility wires, a quick and difficult maneuver.

After the war, a number of locals got their licenses at the Culver City Airport. Former police officer Jack Scholz was licensed on May 4, 1947. Many, like Fred Machado, used the GI Bill to get their commercial licenses. After Fred soloed there in 1947, his interest in planes continued, and years later, he built his own single-seater "Quickie" from a kit along with George Sweeny (former Culver City fire chief). Both men later built and flew their own "Boredom Fighters, too."

The airport was history in 1951. A Mayfair Market opened on the site, and behind it, Sunkist Park became a housing development. The hangar area became an Earl Scheib body shop for a time.

JOE PETRELLI'S AIRPORT CAFE

Joe Petrelli's Airport Cafe was moved to the property known as the Kite site—where Circuit City was located prior to Office Depot and Sprouts.

According to George Petrelli, his uncle Joe slid the first tiny restaurant across Sepulveda in the middle of the night to relocate it. The little cafe was built while Joe was working for the studios. Joe Petrelli died in 1958, two years after George Petrelli came from Italy to work for his uncle in the meat department. The "new" Geo Petrelli's location on Sepulveda Boulevard is the result of a successful redevelopment project in 1995. When you walk in the door, you will find at least one of the three smiling Petrellis, as well as walls of memorabilia highlighting its eighty years in business and Culver City Airport location.

STERN'S FAMOUS BARBECUE

Stern's was located at the west end of Culver City at 12568 West Washington Boulevard. It was established at that location in 1922, which was three years prior to the annexation of the Walnut Park Tract by Culver City. Stern's was founded by immigrant Isadore Stern. As Stern traveled west, his last stop before California was El Paso, Texas, where he established a butcher shop. When times were tough and his meat sales were down, Isadore Stern began to barbecue meats in the back of the shop. To his surprise, he sold more barbecued meat than anything else.

Stern's Barbecue became *the* destination for western-style dining, and over time, Isadore Stern's sons, Max and Edward Stern, became the proprietors.

Stern's Famous Barbecue, opened in 1922, was just that! Sterns catered to many, both at the restaurant at the west end of Culver City and offsite.

Harold Stern became the third-generation owner. In 1982, Stern's Barbecue celebrated its sixtieth anniversary. Although it's since closed, locals still talk about the meals they enjoyed at Stern's. But the greatly enjoyed barbecue sauce and coleslaw recipes remain in the hands of the Stern family!

THE ROLLERDROME

People flocked to Culver City from miles around to skate at the Rollerdrome, which opened in 1928 on Washington Place. The wooden structure was designed with a gently rounded parabola-like roofline, and the resulting height accommodated a mezzanine. Many locals, like Virgie Eskridge, remember Mr. Osterloh, the musician who filled the building with cheery roller-skating music. A bell and instructions to "clear the floor" prepared the rink for a variety of skating opportunities. In a recent interview, Virgie pointed to the Rollerdrome as an example of the freedom children had growing up here in earlier days and just one of many entertainment options.

Old-timer Ethel Ashby described the Rollerdrome as "a grand place to go, just wonderful." Ethel and her fiancé met friends there regularly on Friday nights and sometimes mid-week during the early 1930s. She talked about the variations in skating choices, which included men only, ladies only, singles skate and couples skate. According to Ethel, when it was a call for all men, they often raced around the rink "like a bunch of whippets." The couples skate was her opportunity to learn dancing on roller skates. During singles only, Ethel said it was a time for "the young kids to show off with lots of turns and jumps."

Suitable dress at the Rollerdrome was defined as skirts and blouses for the girls and slacks and pants for the boys. Ethel elaborated that "jeans were for work or hiking" at that time. In later years, women wore pantsuits. Jessie Belford, another local, told stories of going to the Rollerdrome when they got their "Senior Sweaters" at Hamilton High. After skating, that crowd often went to the Sunburst Malt Shop in Downtown Culver City. Jessie described one routine, "Crack the Whip," as treacherous at the end of the line. She also recalled that Washington Place flooded during heavy rains. Once, they opened up one door of their car and "the water just went out the other door."

The Rollerdrome was a welcome addition to Culver City, as seen at the ceremony during construction, which was attended by Culver City mayor Reve Houck (seated in light suit). It was a local meeting place for all ages.

Generations were drawn to enjoy birthday parties at the Rollerdrome. Moms got help from other moms who also skated to manage the group. It must have been a challenge to get each child the correct size rental skates, lace them and keep all of the kids upright!

The Rollerdrome operated until 1970, when termite damage forced its closure. City records show that the demolition of the Rollerdrome occurred in August 1971. The property continued as a recreational space as it transitioned into Tellefson Park in 1976.

The Egyptian House

Stories abound when it comes to the "Egyptian House." This local landmark stood on the creek side of Lucerne Avenue at Lafayette Place.

Many recall the "Egyptian House," which was constructed on Lucerne with its back to the creek. Although the owner/builder never resided in the remarkable structure, many have stories to tell.

The story of its origin is probably the most poignant. According to local lore, the property owner, a Mr. Brown, fell in love with an Egyptian princess. He built a home for his princess on Lucerne Avenue in the 1920s. It was distinctive in architectural design, two stories high with etched windows and gold locks, and all amenities were of the highest quality. There was even an eight-foot-deep circular swimming pool behind the house. Sadly, the princess died on her voyage to America to marry. The distressed Mr. Brown never moved into the house he built for his intended. Although difficult to verify, local craftsmen, like Frank Lugo, spoke of working on the construction of the house and described the gold that was being used to enhance it.

In the official city records, the earliest building permit was issued to a Mr. H.D. Brown. The two-story house in question was located at 9530 Lucerne. It had a basement, one kitchen, many rooms and a swimming pool. If you look closely at the picture, you can see the image of an Egyptian pharaoh next to the front door. City records also contain a 1956 business license application for a permit and variance for a rooming house called Egyptian Manor. The applicant at that time was a Lakewood resident, Carl Steiner, who received both the permit and the variance. In 1957, although the variance was not renewed, the rooming house continued as a residence for its manager and her family, with eight rooms rented out.

There were police reports in 1961 of a drug arrest, and an application to continue the rooming house was denied. That same year, one report indicated that the police interviewed a dozen residents, and all but one living in the house had felony records. By 1963, the structure had deteriorated, and there was interdepartmental correspondence indicating that the premises were a source of concern to the city. Police reported drinking by juveniles and that a "substantial portion of our delinquency problem stems from there." A document from the chief of police, Eugene Mueller, referred to the neighbors as being "up in arms." Other reports cited health issues stemming from the commonly shared kitchen and mattresses and furniture strewn all over the house, including the basement. It was suggested that hazardous conditions made the premises unfit for human occupancy. The "Egyptian House" was subsequently burned in a training exercise by our local fire department.

PICCADILLY'S AND DRAG RACING

When George Barris first agreed to lend his name to the Crusin' Back to the '50s car show in Culver City, the local sponsors set out to find an image of Piccadilly's Drive-In restaurant. Mr. Barris recalled fondly that drag racing began at Piccadilly's. The 3992 Sepulveda Boulevard address was easy to find, but an actual image was another story. Fred Machado was the best bet, and he came through—in a weird twist of fate. It seems that his brother Tom had unearthed an old menu from Piccadilly's, made a copy of the front and used it to send Fred a note. Fred presented his find with a copy and a smile. The posters and T-shirt for the first car show were designed from that image.

When asked about the drive-in restaurant, there was no hesitation. Fred Machado's immediate response was, "Piccadilly's made great burgers!" The guys used to gather there to eat and check out all the "hot rods." Fred clarified that hot rods were either restored older cars or built by people with imagination from ground up but were not the "muscle cars," which are cars like a Dodge Dart or Plymouth production cars. Sprint cars, which raced on oval tracks, also spent time at Piccadilly's, and some race cars arrived on trailers.

Piccadilly's DRIVE-IN

3992 SEPULVEDA BOULEVARD
AT WASHINGTON WAY ★ PHONE S. M. 7-7155

★★★★★★★★★★★★★★★★★★★★★★★★★★★★★★★★★★

Featuring the New

Juicy Jumbo
HAMBURGERS
"A SQUARE MEAL ON A ROUND BUN"
★★★★★★★★★★★★ **25c** ★★★★★★★★★★★★

Two Good Places to Eat!
Here and Home.

Greatly missed by many is Piccadilly's Drive-In, which offered a social atmosphere on Sepulveda Boulevard. The menu from Piccadilly's shows off its unique architecture and draw to the hamburger crowd. *Courtesy of Fred and Tom Machado.*

When questioned about Piccadilly's, Dennis Parrish immediately said, "Best hamburger in town—the sauce was like no other." His wife, Willy, was also appreciative of the shredded lettuce. They both agreed that everyone went to Piccadilly's "just to look at the cars." Dennis described a "chopped and channeled '50 Merc, lower than low...with no doorknobs, no hood ornament, no ID and smoothed off with a beautiful paint job—a light violet." Dennis also remembered that Piccadilly's "had all the best-looking waitresses." Pat (Martin) Clapp said her friends would "qualify around it," which meant driving around to check out the people and cars. After their burgers, usually about 10:00 p.m., the drag racers headed down Culver Boulevard to Centinela. Cars were positioned to block the road so that they could race west. Fred remembers racing one night "until the police chased us out. The cars drove all over the railroad tracks to get away." According to Fred, the location was chosen because there were few homes west of Centinela. Dennis raced his '56 Corvette there and recalls the start and finish line on the street, defining the quarter-mile race. Willy's brother Bill also raced.

There was an earlier component to this drag racing ritual. In 1940, the exercise often started at the Rollerdrome nearby. Some of the guys sporting their "Hell Cats" car club jackets skated at the rink before they headed to Piccadilly's.

Fiesta La Ballona

Fiesta La Ballona began in 1951 as a weeklong celebration of local heritage. Since Culver City was carved primarily from two ranchos, Rancho La Ballona and Rancho Rincón de los Bueyes, the descendants were honored citizens. There was something happening daily during this festive week. Originated by the chamber of commerce, activities were patterned to appeal to every sector of the community. They included contests for the "queen" and her court, a luncheon, a hobby show and even a beard-growing contest for the guys. There was also an antique car show. There were two parades— one down the city streets and one for children at Veterans Memorial Park. Evening events included a square dance, a teen dance and a barbecue. The aquacade in the "new" plunge (1950) drew crowds to a show of synchronized swimming interspersed with clowning antics under the stars.

Above: The early Fiesta La Ballona featured a big parade. The "floats" were labors of fun-loving locals. Pictures like these offer a little extra history, as one can note the businesses in operation during those times. Stella Music is the float sponsor, but note the Hull Building, with Freeman Furniture behind, and other names from the past. *Courtesy of the Freeman Collection.*

Opposite, top: Fiesta La Ballona, created in 1951 by the Culver City Chamber of Commerce, used the new Veterans Memorial Building as just one of the venues for the weeklong celebration of local heritage. Pictured at the microphone is Charles Lugo, a fifth-generation descendant of Francisco Salvador Lugo. Lugo is surrounded by his children, Julie and Carlos, and other descendants on stage, as well as Fiesta La Ballona "royalty"—the queen and her court.

Opposite, bottom: This Fiesta La Ballona photo taken in 1952 depicts local business participants. Ed Tinger (Culver City Flowers) and his wife (center) show off their trophy as Higuera descendant Ela Cheuvront (in Spanish dress and mantilla) looks on with chamber president Firley Cleveland (in hat and serape). *Courtesy of Virgie Tinger Eskridge Collection.*

Everyone was expected to "dress" on Friday. If they didn't, they might end up taking a ride in the "Pokey." A recently opened Culver Center drew crowds to its "Thieves Market," which was essentially a sidewalk sale. Culver Center Street was shut down for that day, with sale proceeds earmarked for charity. There were also window dressing contests and fiesta posters in many retail windows. On the day of the "big parade," locals lined up on Higuera Street, and the parade honored the "early families" with names like Machado, Talamantes, Ybarra, Rocha, Saenz, Higuera and Lugo. The descendants proudly took pains with their costumes. Clarita Marquez Young, an Ybarra and Saenz descendant, had thirteen special dresses with matching mantillas. In an interview in the 1990s, Clarita said, "The early fiestas began in the early 1950s. Their purpose was to celebrate the Spanish first families. I never missed a fiesta—they were like the spice of my life! I rode in the parade, and so did my mother, Senaida Ybarra, and grandmother, Maria Jesus Ybarra."

Clarita went on to become one of the founding members of the Culver City Historical Society and was named its "Madrina," or godmother of the group. Clarita, a constant from the beginning, worked hard to educate the community about the early settlers. She was a member of the Beverly Hills Parlor of the Native Daughters of the Golden West, which placed the marker on our first studio, now Sony Pictures. Ella Cheuvront and family represented the Higueras. Vicenta Lugo, a Machado and Lugo descendant, sewed her own dress with layers of bright red ruffles. She wore her grandmother's Spanish comb in her hair, which was topped with fine lace. She carried a fan, and like most, she relished the festive atmosphere and liked sharing times with her brothers, nieces and nephews. Mothers made costumes for children in the parades, whether for a ceremonial ride in a horse-and-buggy with family or a walk through Veterans Park in costume for the Kiddie Parade. This was the beginning of an awareness of Latin heritage for many. But it also included history from the beginning, from Native Americans to early settlers to cowboys.

Some years the descendants were featured in vintage cars. There was always a placard on the vehicle identifying the family name. People lined the streets and waved as the vehicles passed by. Some never really mastered "the wave." Some were frankly a little shy. Equestrian units shimmering with silver accents included notables like Sheriff Biscaluz and his "posse," and local stuntman Carl Pitti was always on his horse. Marching bands and scout troops moved down the street to the delight of the locals as their families and friends watched for familiar faces. One of the floats carried the Fiesta Queen and her court. One year, the rotary club rode donkeys instead of sponsoring a float. Everyone had fun—that was the key.

The Kiddie Parade took place at the Veterans Memorial Park under the direction of the parks and recreation department. The children were all costumed in heritage garb and rode in or pulled floats crafted by their parents. It was probably a little competitive fun for the parents, who proudly lined the walkway, taking photo after photo as the children moved by. Families could do amazing things to turn red wagons into floats like

Mamacita's Tamale Wagon! The Kiddie Parade winner received a prize ice cream cake to share with family and friends.

The real beauty of those times was that it was inclusive, a little like St. Patrick's Day, when anyone who wants to be Irish *is* Irish. During the Fiesta, all it took was a pair of jeans to dress "western" or a little creativity to dress as Indians (politically correct at the time) or in Mexican or Spanish costumes. Olvera Street probably did a good business in August during those early years. People could do as little or as much as they wanted in the way of costumes. The first year, Firley Cleveland, the manager of the local water company and chair of the chamber of commerce, dressed as a monk—the next year, photos show him wearing a hat and serape.

So, what is a fiesta? Translations of the word could be party, reunion or holiday. The Latinos don't have a corner on partying, but they do have a history of enjoying celebrations. If locals learned anything at all from the early fiestas, it was probably commitment to community and the joy of sharing time and traditions with others.

Rose Parade Floats

The introduction to the *Tournament of Roses Handbook* states:

> *The annual Pasadena Tournament of Roses Parade is hailed as the most photographed and televised annual event in the world. Since the parade's inception in 1889, when parade floats were horse and buggy units, to modern day floats that take a year to construct, the parade has become internationally known as a midwinter burst of color.*

The Pasadena Tournament of Roses Association began in 1895, and this active community-based group boasts about one thousand active volunteer members each year. The tournament's office has records that show that Culver City's first Rose Parade entry was in 1925. In an ad in the December 27, 1927 *Culver City Star News*, locals were reminded of available transportation to the parade. The Pacific Electric Railway stop was next to the Ivy Substation. Subsequent entries appeared in the New Year's parades in 1938, 1939, 1940, 1949 and 1950.

Everyone loves a parade! In the 1980s, Culver City's Business and Convention Center raised funds to enter floats from 1985 to 1988 in the Tournament of Roses Parade. The 1986 "Kings of Comedy" float won the theme trophy, and the 1988 entry "Fantasy on Film" was awarded the director's trophy.

In the second half of the twentieth century, Culver City entered four floats in the Rose Parade. The Culver City Tournament of Roses Association formed to sponsor floats from the city, and the Culver City Convention and Visitors' Bureau spearheaded the efforts. The cost of the floats was borne by the association that raised funds in a variety of ways. For the 1986 entry, for example, there was a special advance screening of *Rocky IV* at the MGM Studios. In September 1986, the group planned a "Fabulous '50s" party at the Fox Hills Mall after hours. This was the fundraiser for the January 1, 1987 entry. All four entries in the 1980s had movie themes, appropriate for the "Heart of Screenland." In 1985, Culver City's float was titled "Premiere." The following year, "Kings of Comedy" won the theme trophy. Culver City entered "Movie Magic" in 1987, and in 1988, "Fantasy on Film" won the director's trophy.

Other Resources: Organizations, Service Clubs and Sister Cities

Culver City is a community with a history of caring people. In addition to the organizations established to support our schools, there are many other groups that have made it a priority to give their time and efforts to make this a wonderful city in which to live and work.

The first organization was the Culver City Woman's Club, which was the idea of early city trustee Clyde Slater. When it began in 1920, it read like the who's who of Culver City ladies. Mrs. Culver was an early president.

Culver City Lions Club was chartered on April 30, 1923, with its first member listed as city founder Harry H. Culver. The Lions motto is "We Serve," and it is the largest service club worldwide. It is heralded for its eyesight screenings, particularly in schools.

The Culver City Rotary Club held its first meeting in Culver City on February 24, 1930. The wheel used in the rotary logo was originally designed to remind the club that its meetings rotated from one member to another. The rotary club donated the Westminster Chimes for the Veterans Memorial Building tower and established the foundation that built Rotary Plaza housing.

The Culver City Exchange Club was chartered in Culver City in 1949. Its focus has been on the youth, and the club has been a generous donor to programs in the schools, from the Child Safety Week programs and Academy of Visual and Performing Arts to reseeding athletic fields and supporting of the Culver City Youth Health Center. It also spearheads the annual Fourth of July Fireworks Show at the high school.

Other clubs include the Culver City Optimist Club, which supported a boys' home and programs on bicycle safety, and the Culver City Kiwanis Club. The Culver City Soroptimist Club, a club for women chartered in 1951, is no longer operating.

There has been a growing list of other organizations that support the community, including the Culver-Palms YMCA. The Culver City Guidance Clinic Guild, which raised funds to support mental health, has transitioned into Didi Hirsch Community Mental Health Center. The sports community includes Little Leagues, American Youth Soccer Organization and Boy Scouts and Girl Scouts at all levels. There are also the Friends of the Library, the Culver City Historical Society, Friends of the Culver City Dog Park and many more.

Culver City recently celebrated the fiftieth anniversary of its Sister City program, which began in 1962. There is a bronze marker on the corner of Culver and Duquesne in front of the entrance to Culver City Hall and a sign that points to all four of our sister cities. The Sister City programs were established under President Dwight D. Eisenhower in 1956. The intent was to offer a "people-to-people" program through which a two-way cultural exchange could take place. It was designed to promote friendship and understanding between the United States and people of other countries. Culver City's Sister City Committee was established in December 1962. The method of establishing a sister-city relationship with Culver City operates on two levels. There must be a vote from the Sister City Committee as well as the city council. Once the agreement has been made, there is usually a visitation scheduled to each city by a delegation that includes members of the Sister City Committee and city officials. A ceremony in each city cements the bond.

The first relationship was established with Uruapan, Michoacán, Mexico, in 1964. Uruapan's population is about 150,000, and the city is known for its active volcano, national park, embroidery, pottery and lacquer work. We have contributed many items (including a used firetruck) to Uruapan and continue to send supplies, such as turnout coats, for their use. The Casa de Cuna orphanage in Uruapan is supported by funds from our Sister City Committee.

Kaizuka, Japan, paired with Culver City in 1965. This has probably been the most active cultural exchange relationship. Kaizuka is located twenty miles south of Osaka and has a population near ninety thousand. The Japanese Meditation Garden in front of the Culver City Library was a gift from Kaizuka in 1974. To celebrate its twenty-fifth anniversary, the Sister City Committee offered a reenactment of the dedication ceremony in 1999. A delegation visited from Kaizuka for the occasion. Culver City commissioned a beautiful sculpture by Natalie Krol (the artist who created the Filmstrip USA) to be installed in Kaizuka's town center. Ongoing visitations include those of a summer middle school student as well as occasional marathon runners (Paul Jacobs, Dan Cohen and Jim Forte).

Our third sister-city relationship began in 1983 with Iksan City, South Korea. Originally known as Iri City, this primarily industrial city of 180,000 plus is located in the Chollabuk-Do province of Korea. Visitations are infrequent.

Lethbridge, Canada, "twinned" with Culver City in 1989. Located in the Rocky Mountains in the province of Alberta, Lethbridge is the sister city of closest size. It has been a very active and reciprocal relationship, and friends stay in one another's homes on visitations. In 1999, a trip was scheduled to celebrate the tenth anniversary of the relationship.

In 1993, Culver City was asked to participate in a sister-city relationship with Yanji City, Jilin, China. Visitations have been rare, and the relationship has been dormant for some time.

Libraries

Our first local library was located in the area of the Ivy Substation/Culver Depot. Later, the library was located on Braddock Drive between Lafayette Place and Duquesne Avenue. Veterans Memorial Park hosted the next library, which was situated between the Veterans Memorial Building and the Plunge. Its central doors in front and back could almost have been called an "attractive nuisance," as high school students, particularly in the '60s, took great pride in riding their bikes or skateboards straight through from the front to the park in back—much to the dismay of the librarians. That building became the first Senior Center and is currently repurposed as a teen center.

In the early 1970s, Culver City's county supervisor, Kenneth Hahn, was planning a new Culver City library to open in 1972. It was opened at 4975

The Culver City Public Library opened in 1972 as a part of the Los Angeles County library system. This early picture shows the new facility before the installation of the Japanese meditation garden, which was a gift from Kaizuka, Culver City's sister city in Japan. The library was renamed after the death of Congressman Julian Dixon in 2000. It has been known as the Culver City Julian Dixon Library since 2005.

Overland Avenue, where it remains today. After the death of our beloved congressman Julian Dixon, it was renamed the Culver City Julian Dixon Library. Visitors have been delighted to enjoy the Japanese meditation garden in front, a donation from our sister city Kaizuka, Japan.

An emerging museum/library district is growing just north of the Culver City Julian Dixon Library. The Culver City Historical Society Archives and Resource Center is housed in the Veterans Memorial Building at Overland and Culver. Across Overland, the Mayme Clayton Library and Museum is another local resource. The Wende Museum plans to move from Fox Hills to the Armory property just behind the Veterans Memorial Park.

GONE BUT NOT FORGOTTEN: THE CULVER CITY REDEVELOPMENT AGENCY

The Culver City Redevelopment Agency (CCRA) was established by the city council in 1971 "to eradicate blight and stimulate economic development and reinvestment." The agency members are the same five council members wearing different hats. The first chair of the agency was Richard Pachtman.

The agency first identified Slauson-Sepulveda and Overland-Jefferson as project areas. A $16.6 million tax allocation bond was issued in 1973 to assist with the Fox Hills Mall. The mall opened in the fall of 1975. It was the first major agency project and continues to bring in a substantial percentage of our sales tax revenue. The next area identified was the Washington-Culver project area. After thirty years, 42 percent of the city's land area is considered redevelopment project area. The CCRA continued its work in the 1970s with the Fox Hills Business Center, Buckingham Heights Business Park and Fox Hills Park. Magic Johnson is still the most famed user of the park's basketball hoops to date.

In the next decade, the agency continued its work with the Corporate Pointe office buildings and town homes. An unanticipated impact of Corporate Pointe's development was a height limit initiative written by Pachtman and passed in 1990. Culver Center's first rehab was completed in 1983, and it has undergone redevelopment as Westside Walk. During the 1980s, there was the acquisition of Cougar Park and competition of the Robertson Business Park and the Meralta Office Plaza. The Meralta Plaza was constructed on the site of an early mixed-use development, the Meralta Theatre, where owners Pearl Merrill and Laura Peralta lived above their theater and could watch movies from their living room bay window. The Rotary Plaza and other senior/low-cost housing was built, and the agency also acquired the Culver Theatre. Neighborhood Preservation Program funding began, and the striking granite Filmland Corporate Center (now Sony Pictures Plaza) was completed in 1986. The Interim City Hall was assembled at the northeast corner of Overland and Culver in 1988, and Mike Miller Toyota was completed the following year.

The 1990s began with the renovation of the Veterans Memorial Building. A new agreement with the Culver City Unified School District to offset the impacts of agency projects was signed. The Watseka and Cardiff Parking structures were built in Downtown Culver City. There were also the Kronenthal Park renovation and the creation of the Downtown and East Washington Façade Improvement Programs. Funding was made available for the Culver Hotel renovation, and a rental assistance program was initiated. Fire Station #1 opened at its new location. The CCRA's 1987 long-term lease with the City of Los Angeles for the Ivy Substation/Media Park was renovated into a welcoming gateway in 1993. Machado Road became a reality, and a Small Business Earthquake Grant program became available. The Culver Studios Office Building opened a block east of the studio.

Culver City's new city hall opened in 1995 and looks changed with a new Downtown Streetscape and a Farmers Market. There were Higuera Street improvements, the Kite Site redevelopment and the relocation of Petrelli's. Improvements were made in the Hayden Tract, and gap-closer loans were made available. Howard Industries was built and the award-winning Washington Streetscape was completed, as was the police station expansion. Town Plaza redevelopment plans were also approved.

Since 2000, the sun has set on the Studio Drive-In, but it has yielded the Classics at Heritage Park and the new Kayne Eras Center. Miller Honda opened in downtown and Best Buy at Westside Walk. The Beacon Laundry Building is part of the Helms Furniture District, the new Senior Center was opened on the northwest corner of Overland and Culver and, in 2004, the Culver Theatre reopened as a performing arts venue, the Center Theatre Group's Kirk Douglas Culver Theatre. All of these efforts encouraged "private redevelopment," such as the Helms Furniture District, and the redevelopment of both remaining historic studio lots.

Today, Culver City remains the "Heart of Screenland," with many of our star features being products of the Culver City Redevelopment Agency. Unfortunately, the state eliminated redevelopment agencies in 2012.

HISTORIC SITES

When the Culver City Historical Society was incorporated in 1980 under founding president Cathy Zermeno, it began a program of marking historic sites, the first one being the site of the 1928 city hall. To qualify, sites must be at least fifty years old and historically significant.

The first marking, the site of the 1928 city hall, took place in 1981, ten years prior to the adoption of our city's Historic Preservation Ordinance. Charles Lugo was the first Historic Sites chair. The markers are traditionally bronze plaques, some mounted in concrete, some on the structures. Following are markings by the Culver City Historical Society to date:

> HISTORIC SITE NO. 1: The 1928 City Hall
> HISTORIC SITE NO. 2: The Hull Building
> HISTORIC SITE NO. 3: St. Augustine's Church
> HISTORIC SITE NO. 4: The Citizen Building
> HISTORIC SITE NO. 5: The Legion Building
> HISTORIC SITE NO. 6: Main Street
> HISTORIC SITE NO. 7: The Culver Studios
> HISTORIC SITE NO. 8: The Lugo Ranch
> HISTORIC SITE NO. 9: The Helms Building
> HISTORIC SITE NO. 10: La Ballona School
> HISTORIC SITE NO. 11: Camp Latham
> HISTORIC SITE NO. 12: Victory/Dr. Paul Carlson Park
> HISTORIC SITE NO. 13: Veterans Memorial Building

In the 1980s, Culver City directed that a survey of historic structures be completed. A Historic Preservation Advisory Committee was formed, and the final document, completed by Thirtieth Street Architects, was adopted by the Culver City Council in 1991. A Cultural Affairs Commission was appointed by the council in 2000, which folded Historic Preservation and Art in Public Places together. In 2004, the required plaques were ordered and installed on historic structures. Oval city plaques were placed on historic structures designated by the city as having "landmark" or "significant" status.

ABOUT THE AUTHOR

J ulie Lugo Cerra is a sixth-generation Californian and a Culver City native who enjoys being called the "accidental historian." She was appointed official city historian by the Culver City Council in 1996. As a past president of the Culver City Historical Society, she is still active on the society board as the museum vice-president, working on educational programs and tours, as well as giving lectures and presentations on state and local history.

Cerra continues to enjoy a high degree of community involvement, having served on Culver City Board of Education, Cultural Affairs Commission, Culver City Chamber of Commerce, Historic State Capitol Commission and the Friends of the Library. She also served as a past president of the Culver City Sister Cities Committee. She maintains membership in organizations such as the Historical Society of Southern California, Los Angeles Conservancy, Los Californianos and the Los Angeles City Historical Society and is grateful for the many recognitions she has received for her volunteer work.

After Cerra graduated from California State University–Northridge with a BA in sociology, she established her own consulting business, which deals with private/public partnerships, land use projects, public art and historic preservation issues. Being semi-retired gives her time to enjoy being "Grandma Julie" and other pleasantries like cooking, gardening and a variety of creative pursuits. Cerra has written 450 articles for the *Culver City News* and has supplied historical information for the Culver City and Culver City Historical Society websites. This is her fifth book.